Manage Your Content and Devices

Learn The Secrets of Android and Unlock The Full Potential of Smartphones, Tablets and Smart Watches

ORVILLE CAROL FRED

© Copyright 2021 – Orville Carol Fred All rights reserved.

The content contained within this book may not be reproduced, duplicated or transmitted without direct written permission from the author or the publisher. Under no circumstances will any blame or legal responsibility be held against the publisher, or author, for any damages, reparation, or monetary loss due to the information contained within this book. Either directly or indirectly.

Legal Notice

This book is copyright protected. This book is only for personal use. You cannot amend, distribute, sell, use, quote or paraphrase any part, or the content within this book, without the consent of the author or publisher.

Disclaimer Notice

Please note the information contained within this document is for educational and entertainment purposes only. All effort has been executed to present accurate, up to date, and reliable, complete information. No warranties of any kind are declared or implied.

Readers acknowledge that the author is not engaging in the rendering of legal, financial, medical or professional advice. The content within this book has been derived from various sources.

Please consult a licensed professional before attempting any techniques outlined in this book. By reading this document, the reader agrees that under no circumstances is the author responsible for any losses, direct or indirect, which are incurred as a result of the use of information contained within this document, including, but not limited to, — errors, omissions, or inaccuracies.

Discover 7 Magnificent Things you can do with your Android Phone

Click the link or use the QR code below

https://bit.ly/3gXvkOy

Table of Contents

Introduction 9
Chapter 1: Overview of my Devices 13
    Overview Of An Android Device 14
    Setting up your new Android phone 15
    Phone Backup Protocol 19
    The navigation buttons and gestures 20
    Multiple screens 23
    The Notification Shade 24
    Quick Settings bar 25
    Basic Android Applications 26
    Extensive customization 29
    Google Pay and Google Play 31
    A unified Google experience 32
    Android setbacks 33
    Battery and Its life 35
    Inconsistent updates 35
Chapter 2: History of Smart Devices 37
    Early smartphones 41
Chapter 3: Comparing between devices 45
    What is a smartphone 47
    What is a cell phone 47
    The Difference in Smartphones And Cellphones 48
    How Do Smartphones Work? 51
    About Featured Phones 52
Chapter 4: Comparing Between Operating Systems 53
    Features of an Andriod Device 57

Chapter 5: Managing your Mobile Phone 61
   Finding the Best Cell Phone Plan 62
   Choosing the Right Phone 66
   Making Adequate Use Of Your Cell Phone 68

Chapter 6: Managing your smartphone and Tablet 75
   Configure Your Lock Screen 76
   Disabling Bloatware 76
   Finding Your Phone 77
   Mobile Data Tracking 78
   Do Not Disturb Settings 78
   Digital Wellbeing 79
   Back Up Photos 79
   "OK Google" Voice Prompt 80
   Use of Google Assistant 80
   Making use of your device's Screen Pinning 81
   The use of Swipe Input on the Keyboard of your device 81
   Applying different power modes using the Power-Saving mode of your device 82
   System Dark Theme 82
   Using your device Manager to Manage Default Applications 83
   Setting up Developer Options 83

Chapter 7: Managing your smart watch 85
   Connecting To An Android Device 88
   Setting Up a Smartwatch 90
   Customizing a Smartwatch 90
   Basic Smartwatch Apps 91

Chapter 8: Unlocking the full potential of your devices 95
   Blocking calls from people you don't want 96

Turning your phone into a hotspot 96

Unlocking your phone with just a Bluetooth device 97

Opening the visited Web pages in your web browser when you have no internet connection. 97

How to decrease or increase the font size of your 98

Listen to any radio network for free. 98

How to find or wipe the data of a lost phone. 99

How to connect your smart device to a mouse, or a keyboard or an SD card reader. 99

Turning your old phone into a real security camera. 100

Unlock the full potential of your Android device through Rooting 100

What then is Rooting? 101

Rooting and benefits that come with it 101

Rooting and risks that comes with it 102

Chapter 9: Controlling Your devices remotely 103

Setting up the Android TV Remote Control app 104

Adding another User to Your Android Tablet 105

Remotely controlling your PC. 107

Chapter 10: Making certain basic installations 109

Downloading Applications from Google Play 111

Downloading Applications from other places 112

Downloading From Sideloading Apps 113

Third-Party App Stores 115

Downloading Apps From Your PC 116

Chapter 11: Improving your productivity with your devices 119

Chapter 12: Being safe with your devices 127

Do Avoid long conversation 128

Make use of headset options 128
Keep mobile devices away from the body 129
Turn off Your WiFi and Cellular data 129
Avoid Making calls at low signals 130
Make fewer calls, send More Texts 130
Use landline telephones rather 131
Keep phone away from children's reach 131
Radiation protection accessories 132
The place of Safe Charging 132
Measures to avoid Device Fraud 133
Conclusion 135

Thanks again for choosing this book. It is my first book and I'd really love to hear your thoughts.

Make sure to leave a short review on Amazon if you enjoy it.

https://www.amazon.com/review/create-review

Introduction

Mobile devices have made a tremendous change to our world. Those days of caring bulky laptops and cumbersome desktops around have finally come and gone. Flamboyant smartphones and awesome tablets have now come to stay, mobile devices today have made business transactions be done so quickly. Those big and mighty computers have been replaced by this very new generation of super-thin and powerful devices of several shapes and sizes. Also, it is something to be happy about that this new technology has an all-day long battery life with it, enabling us to remain productive no matter the place we happen to go to or the things we happen to be doing.

These devices have now been made the intrinsic part of everyday living and livelihood of man, employees can now be using their device at work even as employers makes use of theirs, no one can stop them not to. This brought in the idea of 'bring your own device' (BYOD) — a culture which is rising so high and is aimed to make the very task of everyone easier, considering how mobile devices could tightly fit into several business and establishments, forming an essential part of work. However, although Mobile Devices are useful in our day to day business activities, but some people misuse them, they fail to understand it's functionality and usefulness.

So in this awesome book, we have compiled a very comprehensive and understandable guide to becoming more skilled at using your devices—starting from your GSM (your Mobile Phone) to your iOS device, then your Android phone, tablet, and even your smartphone watch. We've compiled together this smart and comprehensive guide to help everyone who is using smart devices as a platform and the various important functions of these devices. You will also be guided brilliantly on this book for you to get a detailed knowledge to choose a list of the best smartphones and smartwatches as you go to the market to purchase them, you can have a better idea and explicit knowledge of the Android world, the iOS ecosystem, the tablet devices and the smart watches too.

Section 1

Chapter 1: Overview of my Devices

Mobile devices and Mobile applications enable people within their workplaces and businesses to complete some basic and specific tasks and manage them efficiently. We are now living in the days where almost all things are possible on a mobile device, and it largely possess several features and capabilities just as a PC to be used for effective work. Some instances of the business jobs and certain tasks you can undertake with a mobile device include the following:

- Manipulating and editing office documents
- Using a to-do lists to track progress
- Making implementation of a GTD methodology — also known as get things done methodology.
- Manipulating and organizing business accounts
- Using the Calendar and managing appointments
- Managing certain Projects
- Communication on an Individualistic, group and team basis
- Video Editing and imagery
- The place of Podcasts

Let us look into these devices briefly using the Android device as a case study.

Overview Of An Android Device

One important Operating System there is in the world of technology is actually the Android Operating system. Android as an Operating System grants us the offer of more advanced flexibility for developers — for those who want to customize and set up the very way in which their Operating System appears and functions. This Operating System is very highly customizable if you can only know the actual basics of Technical Education. It is so useful if you would love to develop an application, especially if you want to dive right into application development.

Going from the point of using an iPhone to the point of using an Android device can be a bit quarreling. You really may not be able to get the true Android experience in which Google as a company intended. On the other hand, you will not see the same unification as can be seen in messaging over devices. On the other hand, however, you will probably experience the very same in-app restrictions, and this gives you even much more freedom of purchase than you could possibly have—or had—on an iPhone device.

If you actually choose to jump onto the Android campaign for the very first time, or you want to get to know a lot about Android devices and their ecosystem, there is such a whole lot for you to figure out. So, let's get to know more about a new Android phone.

Setting up your new Android phone

For you to start doing anything on your new Android Phone, you actually need first to switch the new phone on and as it is on, you set it up. So down below, I will show you a whole list of what you need to do as soon as you receive the very first greeting on your welcome screen—We'll look at an overview of your device from there.

First Step: After the welcome screen, the very next thing you'll see is the language settings. You first need to select a language of choice and as soon as you're done choosing the language, just click on the Start button or link close by.

Second Step: After that, you will need to connect to your network service center—to your mobile network, and this you can do by inserting the SIM card into the sim card port—also known as a sim card slot. You may need to skip this step if you want to do the sim card installation later or right there in the right place already.

Third Step: The next thing to do is connect your device to a local wireless network—Local Area Network (LAN)—by class clicking on the network link in the next step after the sim card settings and then entering the password to the WIFI connection.

Fourth Step: In this next step, you need to set up your device as a new phone, other than that, you can also choose to copy apps and their data from any old device as a means of backup to that old phone. If it was the latter voice you made, then there are three basic methods: Connecting the older phone through the use of a simple USB cable, or by grabbing a backup stored in Google Drive, or even by transferring data from any iPhone device. Then, this very last method will lead you to https://www.android.com/switch — you can decide to visit the website and follow the process.

N/B: Some of the instructions that are remaining — assuming you're restoring from a backup — can be found on the website which it's URL is elucidated above. Then, if it is a new device, you need to skip to the Eighth step.

Fifth Step: You then afterwards need to log onto your Google Account. Let's say you have never got an account with Google; all you just need to do as an escape route is for you to click on the "Get an Account" link and diligently follow all the underlying instructions. Look, on a technical basis, you do not have any need for a Google account in order for you to make adequate use of your phone. Still, it is highly required of truth if you want to download certain apps, or you want to back up your data, or even because you want to use other Google apps and services. Moreover, manufacturers of mobile devices such as the Samsung Company, Tecno, or Itel may ask you if you really want to create a specific or special manufacturer account. Still, you may not need to unless you want to use that company's services as well.

Sixth Step: If you are using a cloud backup, you need to select your service from the list, which you will do if it happens to be more than one. You then may need to put in the PIN that is associated with that very backup.

Seventh Step: You then need to make a selection of what you really want to restore, and as soon as you have done that, selecting your Applications, Contacts, your SMS and Messaging backup, then the settings of your previous device, or even the history of your Call log.

Eighth Step: The next step here is setting up the date and the time of your device.

Ninth Step: After that, you then need to choose and Agree to the legal terms and services of Google.

Tenth Step: Soon after that, you then need to set up the Lock Screen of your device, either using a PIN or a pattern, or even a password. You will need this whenever your face recognition or even your fingerprint scanning fails to work properly.

Eleventh Step: The next set up to be made is the fingerprint scanner or the face recognition setting (actually, the Face), or it can ever be both. To set up the fingerprint scanner, what you just need to do is for you to simply place your finger on the finger print sensor of your device for multiple times until you register your digit. It can either be your thumb or your index finger, or it can even be your middle finger, ring finger, or little finger. Anyone can serve.

Twelfth Step: The very next thing for you to do is for you to set up the Google Assistant of your device to assist you in operations such as making phone calls, serving for answers online, or setting a to-do list.

Thirteenth Step: You also need to set up Google Pay, although it can be optional.

As soon as you have set up your device, the next thing you can do is check if there is any software update for any security patches and all that. Let me take you through on how to get that done in any stock Android 11. Let's go;

First Step: Firstly, you need to swipe right down from the very top bar (or area) of your device for you to expand the shade of the notification of your device, and after that, you need to tap the gear icon.

Second Step: The next thing for you to do is for you to tap on System as you keep scrolling.

Third Step: Then, the next step is for you to tap on Advanced as soon as you are inside the system tab.

Forth Step: Here, you need to tap on System Update right on the advanced tab.

Fifth Step: The next thing to do is click on the Check for Update link or button. Your Android device will then have to check to see if there are any available updates. If there are, you can then download and then install them.

Phone Backup Protocol

As soon as you have moved in successfully, you need to be sure it is backing up your Google Drive. Let me take you through how you can make that check;

First Step: The first thing you need to do is swipe right down from the very top bar or top section of your device to expand the Notification Shade therein and then tap the gear icon there.

Second Step: Secondly, you need to click on the System tab as stated in the last step.

Third Step: You then need to go ahead and navigate the Backup tab located at the system section.

Fourth Step: You need to make sure that you back up to Google drive, so you must check through and make sure that the Back Up to Google Drive is switched on.

N/B: The protocol of Backing up photos and videos is a process that is different from this very one and will be done using the Google Photos application.

The navigation buttons and gestures

By default, your stock Android 11 does not come with it any navigational button, it rather needs to be done manually. You only have a Home button—whether it be a notch or any other structure or icon—that also serves as a stranger handle for your device's applications. Also, there are other times when you will see a back button. The home button generally is visible only for navigation. Anyways, possibly, you can toggle very well on the previous and former three-button navigation system. Let us see how that can be done;

First Step: The first thing for you to do here is for you to Swipe down from the top section of your device in order for you to expand the Notification Shade, and as soon as you do that, you then need to click on the gear icon.

Second Step: The next thing for you to do is click on the System tab to release the things inside it.

Three Step: You then need to click on the Gestures tab located inside the system tab.

Four Step: You then need to click on the System Navigation right there to set it up.

Five Step: As soon as you have chosen, you have to click on the circle next to 3-Button Navigation.

Android device Manufacturers always equip the Android devices that they have manufactured with the three-button navigation system bellow all other options. They also use additional gesture controls. Let me give you an explanation of each button.

Back button: You can return to the very last action you took by pressing the back button found on the bottom bar. Depending on the app you used, it may either have been the things you did in it or just reverting to the last page of your mobile browser. While your browser is running, hold down the button. It will automatically open up a menu that can make it easy to access your favorite bookmarks that you have saved already, as well as your browsing history and even the sites that you visit the most. A Samsung smartphone has this exact button at the top and it defaults to be on the right-hand side, but if you navigate to the Settings, you can choose to move it to the left hand side. Upon entering the choose Display settings and then navigate to Navigation Bar, you can set it up how you wish.

You can appreciate the Home button next in the navigation. Now, the home button of your Android device is at the center of the button bar. By pressing this button, you will be taken directly back to your home screen. So you just need to click on the home button to get to your home screen without getting frustrated and constantly hitting the back arrow key and closing programs just to get to the home screen. You can activate the Google Assistant beautiful by holding the home button down on the latest Android device.

Overview button: You can explore through all dynamic and open applications on your Android gadget with a straightforward tap on the Outline button, which shows up on the upper right half of the base bar. By doing this, you can explore through them rapidly, and hop starting with one application then onto the next quickly. It is feasible to hop straight once more into your most as of late utilized application by twofold tapping on this catch. In each Savvy Samsung telephone, you will track down this very catch on the extremely left hand side, yet you may choose to change the situation of this catch by exploring to the telephone's Settings. You can change the route bar just after getting into the telephone's settings on the Showcase page. Once there, you can pick the format that suits you.

To wrap things up, a few gadgets—explicitly Android telephones—may have certain motion route includes that are empowered naturally, pointed toward wiping out all on-screen route controls. Here's a model: on an Android 11 fundamental gadget, on the off chance that you swipe up from any of the applications recorded beneath, it quickly moves you back home. You can switch between applications by swiping up from the base, holding it down as you swipe, and by delivering only a tad, you would then be able to switch applications.

Practically any Samsung gadget can be controlled with motions rather than catches. On the off chance that you need to get back to the landing page, you simply need to swipe up from the base place, you simply need to swipe up from the base left for the Outline work, then, at that point, you can swipe up from the base appropriate for the Back work. Following these means will permit you to turn on any signal controls you wish. Explore to the Settings part of your telephone to do this. The route bar can be arranged as wanted once you are in the settings of your telephone. You can begin by going to the Showcase and afterward proceeding onward to the Route Bar.

Basically, there is no limitation about the maker with regards to altering contribution for most Android telephones across this specific spot.

Multiple screens

With the Android working framework, you can completely oversee, get to and use a phenomenal exhibit of various showcases - even up to five preceding the KitKat update and as numerous as you need. For example, Android's Home screen used to be focused on a piece, something like a work area, yet as of now, the Google Feed is situated to one side, while the Home screen is fittingly situated to its nearby right. As a result, it creates the impression that any remaining screens are to one side of the Home screen.

In Android gadgets, Clients of these gadgets are perfect for making easy routes, or even gathering applications that are totally held together inside organizers, you can likewise change the backdrop or make changes to the on-screen application dispersing — actually known as the matrix — or then again, change the style of writings on your gadget — textual style changes, shading settings, and application shape arrangement —, etc. You can really make, resize, and even mastermind different gadgets, which show genuine time data from applications and may even be intelligent. These instruments are effectively open by long pushing on any screen.

All applications are available through the Application Cabinet of any android gadget, and this dwells far away at the lower part of each screen — albeit the Google Feed isn't among. Be that as it may, you can generally drag application easy routes right to the screens on the off chance that you would prefer not to manage the application cabinet. Afterward, you can stuff them into envelopes, similar to Study, Games, Work, news, etc.

The Notification Shade

You truly need to swipe down from your gadget's exceptionally top bar, and here you will see the Notice Shade. The notice conceal is the place where you'll see the most movement, as applications broadcast their warnings in a stack. At the top, you'll track down the Fast Settings bar, which you can likewise grow by hauling down its "handle." On Samsung telephones, this handle can't be seen.

In both stock Android and Samsung telephones, you'll track down an Unmistakable connect to excuse all warnings on the shade. You'll likewise see Oversee — as utilized by a large portion of the Android gadget or Notice Settings — as utilized by Samsung makers to deal with these warnings. Finally, for you to overlay the Notice Shade back to the top, the spot it's intended to be, then, at that point, you simply need to tap on the Home catch.

For you to excuse any notice, then, at that point you need to long press and slide it towards the left. You can likewise attempt to tap on the warning. As you do as such, it will trigger an interaction that will open the parent application, or yet still, you can tap on the Unmistakable or Clear All connection at the actual lower part of the shade.

Quick Settings bar

Again, this bar is an advantageous path for somebody to get to the most utilized highlights which he utilizes for the most part from his gadget on the fly. It generally gives exactly the same experience across all the essential Android gadgets. It really frames perhaps the most significant and the most-utilized parts of the Android experience. It shows an extremely slight update with every one of the new form of stock Android while a few makers do have any significant bearing custom changes.

Additionally, there is a space for you that you can really get to this bar even without growing the entire Warning Shade by swiping directly down from the top just by utilizing both of your fingers — most likely, the pointer and the center finger. Likewise, when you genuinely extend the Fast Settings board, it will appear to get jam-pressed brimming with a few fastens that can be appropriately tapped by crossing over or through a couple of pages. Simply swipe left or option to explore these pages.

These catches are so straightforward and simple to utilize. On the off chance that you need to switch through something, you need to turn it on or off, one of these things that requirements flipping is a Wi-Fi organization or even a Bluetooth association, all your simply need to do is only for you to tap on the symbol at the same time. On the off chance that you truly need to completely get to the settings of the capacity actually like getting to the Bluetooth or the Wi-Fi settings of your gadget, you simply need to long-push on the very catch as it shows up there until the individual board shows up. This technique will really save you a ton of time simply by giving you a full and direct admittance to those very settings against what your will go through in tapping through different classifications in that.

This Fast Settings bar does give a slider to darkening and furthermore lighting up the screen. For example, Samsung gadgets do have an extra switch for you to turn on Open air Mode that really lights up the screen to its most extreme for around 15 minutes.

At last, here, you need to realize that for the most part, Android gadgets furnishes it with a stuff symbol that can open the gadget settings. Then, at that point, the pencil symbol there permits you to roll out specific improvements and alter the Speedy Settings bar so you can travel and furthermore erase the catches only appropriately on a case by case basis. Samsung additionally adds a hunt apparatus, then, at that point, a speedy admittance to the force off-screen, and a way to change the catch request and generally format.

Basic Android Applications

The inquiry you might need to pose to now may presumably be; what android applications would it be a good idea for me to get and run on my gadget? All things considered, this is totally dependent upon you. Notwithstanding, there truly are some fundamental applications you ought to consider. Here are a few of them.

Social:

- Facebook,
- Instagram
- Facebook Messenger,
- WhatsApp
- Twitter,

Music:

- Amazon Music
- Spotify,
- Pandora,

Video:

- Netflix,
- Amazon Prime Video,
- HBO Max,
- Hulu,
- Disney+,
- Vudu

Work:

- Microsoft Teams,
- Grammarly Keyboard
- Asana,
- Zoom,
- Slack,

Cloud:

- Dropbox,
- OneDrive,
- Box

Shopping:

- Sam's Club,
- Walmart,
- Amazon,
- Target

Genuinely, you may truly be deprived of getting a couple of good games to play, you need to go experience or go psyche breaking, you need a game on those extremely long flights. Likewise, Microsoft and Sony give the overall population and Android clients applications to stream their control center. Thus, you can really choose to stream on your Android gadget alongside different applications which are console-related.

Extensive customization
Gboard keyboard

The modifying part of an Android gadget has its actual centrality and furthermore its own weaknesses. Take this case, numerous producers are not placed into a furious strain to utilize the attachment UI of Google's stock UI plan.

At any rate, the actual piece of Android gadgets that arrangement with settings and customization likewise makes end clients ready to make and reproduce their encounters, they can tailor and retailor it. Each and every maker which is outside Google engineers do introduce a custom launcher, and this is basically a skin for the Home screen that changes the UI of the App Drawer, and it does give various symbols in the alternate application route just as textual styles, and furthermore adds custom gadgets and a couple of different things. It really doesn't absolutely make change to all the Android UI — which depends on the producer's Android alteration. You can bring a Launcher as a work area subject to your psyche to comprehend it better.

In spite of the fact that you are consistently free to introduce any outsider launcher, the very launchers that are made by Google designers or the producers of your gadget, for example, Tecno or Samsung, are the essential launchers and they truly do a very great job of permitting you to mastermind your substance in an appealing manner.

However, in the event that you can't help thinking that you do require a novel encounter, then, at that point by introducing any outsider launcher will truly be a splendid approach. How about we take the Nova Launcher and Apex Launcher as an occasion here. They do give a remarkable two incomprehensibly various methods of utilizing the stage, every one of them is enhanced with its own showcase feel and route segments.

Then, at that point outside the default launcher, Android likewise allows its client to have the option to set up and modify a significant number of the essential parts. A portion of these essential customizations incorporates permitting clients to redo a huge number like setting the default program and afterward taking out the on-screen console. The last may appear to be a little component on its actual surface, however picking a legitimate Android console from Google Play is in reality, vital to making your Android experience a productive and adorable one in fact.

About Google Assistant

The accessibility of Google Assistant is similar to all Android gadgets that are running Marshmallow 6.0 or later. However, the rendition of the Android Operating framework has one exceptionally significant addition over each and every other versatile working framework, and that is really the very web search tool. Thus, albeit by and large — not in every one — Google Assistant is a more complete asset than Siri.

How about we take a case, Google Assistant will really utilize your pursuit history to show the significant and valuable news, stories and even games scores. It likewise will examine your movement propensities to raise travel data that will be so pertinent to you while furthermore giving you a period gauge and the best bearings for heading to your next area. Google Assistant will even need to disclose the exact second when to leave not to miss your next arrangement.

With the end goal for you to get to Google Assistant on your Android gadget, you simply need to long push on the Home catch of your Android gadget. Before long as you do that, you then, at that point, can likewise initiate it with your voice by utilizing the "Alright, Google" or "Hello Google" voice orders. On the off chance that those orders are not working as expected the manner in which they truly need to work, or if by your own self, you really prefer to change the settings of the highlights of Google Assistant.

Google Pay and Google Play Android Pay

Google Pay is really an awesome stage that truly binds together the Android experience further. Actually, like each and every other portable installment administration empowered on brilliant gadgets, it permits you to make a capacity of actual gift vouchers, utilize a dedication card, or even compensation for things available, thus substantially more. Presently, I need to take you through a great guide on Google Pay and assist you with getting familiar with its set up. In this way, how about we move;

All things considered, Google Pay comes in numerous gadgets being preloaded beforehand, despite the fact that you can have the option to make a download from the Android play store in the event that it turns out that your telephone doesn't have the application pre-introduced in it, Google Play Store is an extremely superb alternative to make the download and establishment.

Assuming as of now, you have a card in your Google Account, all you simply need to do is for you to affirm the subtleties for you to have the option to add it to Google Pay. Then again, you can decide to on the other hand, add a pristine card from any of the banks they are members of simply by snapping an image of your card and affirming every one of the subtleties that are required.

Google Play

The Android comparable to Apple's App Store is the Android Google Play Store, it completely works as the advanced authority store of Google portable organization. It permits clients to buy applications or books, or even motion pictures, and considerably more assets with only a couple of basic taps. It even offers you the exceptionally wonderful chance to introduce distant applications and others and introduce them distantly. Of course, your really implies that you can have the option to download an application on your Mobile tablet gadget when you're busy working and it'll be there when you arrive at your home as well.

A unified Google experience

Android as an innovative stage is a different stage. It isn't restricted constantly to a specific gadget. It isn't just introduced on cell phones, however, it shows up on tablets as well, likewise on set-top-boxes, and furthermore can be introduced on savvy watches, and can likewise be introduced even in Google Glass. You will likewise be stunned to focus on it, seeing it running in an emulator on the Operating System created by Chrome designers, and it is known as Chrome OS. You can likewise consider it to be it is adding Android Applications backing to Google's web-driven working framework, which is for workstations and work areas. Android additionally can be seen being upheld by Windows 10, it likewise permits clients to match their Android telephones in other to settle on decisions, and to likewise send instant messages, or in any event, for them to recover their photographs, and furthermore have the option to see their notices directly on a Windows PC — Operating your Android gadget from the PC like you were working your telephone

In any case, Google—of no uncertainty—is the essential establishment. Google remains between the Chrome program which is introduced on various gadgets and scaffolds it. Google connects between Android telephones and savvy gadgets like Chrome-cast and Google Home, it can even consolidate to each other. Google additionally explores at whatever point you associate an Android telephone to a vehicle with Android Auto. Android is a significant segment in the general administrations of Google as an organization first drive that is open on all stages. What Google does need as a stage is a genuinely brought together informing experience round across gadgets as seen on Apple's items.

Android setbacks

In reality, no Operating System is immaculate, No OS is great, and there are a couple of issues with Android gadgets that can truly be seen and felt. Albeit all the accommodation and the secluded highlights. Android is an open stage, and there are inescapable of a stalwart given the plenty of makers making Android gadgets. A spending Android telephone running a more seasoned adaptation of the stage offers a drastically unexpected involvement compared to the most recent blazing you on Samsung lead. Fortunately, most issues have pretty simple arrangements.

Likewise, one other significant issue that can be knowledgeable about the Android Operating framework is side-stacking. Dissimilar to gadgets fabricated by Apple — Devices are having iOS as their Operating System — Users of Android telephones and gadgets can really introduce applications that are made accessible external Google play store and this is known as side-load. An example of such applications that can be gotten to and introduced out of the Google play store is Fortnite. Presently, the issue turns into that in introducing these unstable applications, you should realize that they can be extremely hazardous since they're screened outside the Google play store, such, there will be no stage to help these Applications and your gadget as well. One of these stages to help your gadget and the application you introduced is Google play secure, which just is accessible in the Google play store, and those applications could have potential malware that can take your data, similar to charge card numbers and record passwords. So consistently be cautious when side-stacking Android applications, and I said, consistently!

Battery and Its life

Android gadgets have not been the actual sort of Operating System that accompanies it an extremely Long Battery Life as its solid suit, however it is currently improving. The majority of the new gadgets within recent memory come introduced in it, a stage like force saving modes just as charge utilizing a straightforward USB-C link — the extremely kind which you can discover almost anyplace. Additionally, a large number of the best Android telephones likewise support remote charging as well.

Inconsistent updates

It's very shocking that each client is helpless before the makers of Android gadgets, particularly regarding getting the most recent updates. Do you think about a stock Android gadget, similar to the Pixel, in the event that you think about it and really, you truly need the most recent Android flavor when it is being delivered. But, then, the Pixel line of telephones is the authority cell phone scope of Google as an organization is ensured steady updates.

The disadvantage to these conflicting updates isn't simply passing up the most current highlights, yet on the very security hazard. The significant hacks like the Stage-fear just as the Heart-drain have incited Google to act with month to month security patches for gadgets, however numerous producers and even transporters do a slow down of those updates, which will presently bring about large number of weak Android telephones.

Chapter 2: History of Smart Devices

A smart device is a useable device that combines mobile phone and computing functions into one form. They are different from feature phones by their stronger hardware capabilities and extensive operating system, which helps wider software, the internet (including browsing on social media such as; Facebook, Instagram.), and multimedia functions (including music, video, cameras, and gaming), alongside the main phone functions such as calls and text messages. Smartphones typically contain several of metal–oxide–semiconductor (MOS) integrated circuit (IC) and it supports wireless communications protocols (such as Bluetooth, Wi-Fi).

Early cell phones were advertised fundamentally towards the endeavor market, endeavoring to connect the usefulness of independent individual computerized colleague (PDA) gadgets with help for cell communication, yet were restricted by their massive structure, short battery life, moderate, simple cell organizations, and youthfulness of remote information administrations. These issues were ultimately settled with the outstanding scaling and scaling down of MOS semiconductors down to sub-micron levels (Moore's law), the improved lithium-particle battery, quicker computerized versatile information organizations (Edholm's law). In addition, more develop programming stages that permitted cell phone environments to grow freely of information suppliers.

During the 2000s, NTT DoCoMo's I-mode stage, BlackBerry, Nokia's Symbian stage, and Windows Mobile started acquiring market foothold, with models regularly including QWERTY consoles resistive touchscreen info, and underscoring admittance to push email and remote web. Following the rising notoriety of the iPhone in the last part of the 2000s, most of the cell phones have highlighted slim, a record like structure factors, with enormous, capacitive screens with help for multi-contact motions instead of actual consoles, and offer the capacity for clients to download or buy extra applications from a unified store, and use distributed storage and synchronization, remote helpers, just as portable installment administrations. Thus, cell phones have to a great extent supplanted PDAs and handheld/palm-sized PCs.

Improved equipment and quicker remote correspondence (because of principles like LTE) have reinforced the development of the cell phone industry. In the second from last quarter of 2012, one billion cell phones were being used around the world. Worldwide cell phone deals outperformed the marketing projections for include telephones in mid 2013.

The improvement of the cell phone was empowered by a few key mechanical advances. The dramatic scaling and scaling down of MOSFETs (MOS semiconductors) down to sub-micron levels during the 1990s–2000s (as anticipated by Moore's law) made it conceivable to fabricate compact keen gadgets, for example, cell phones, just as empowering the progress from simple to quicker computerized remote portable organizations (prompting Edholm's law). Other significant empowering factors incorporate the lithium-particle battery, a vital fuel source empowering long battery life, concocted during the 1980s and popularized in 1991, and the advancement of more developed programming stages that permitted cell phone environments to grow information suppliers freely.

In the mid 90s, IBM engineer Frank Canova understood that chip-and-remote innovation was getting adequately little to use in handheld gadgets. The principal economically accessible gadget that could be appropriately alluded to as a "cell phone" started as a model called "Fisher" created by Canova in 1992 while at IBM and exhibited in November of that year at the COMDEX PC industry career expo. A refined rendition was promoted to purchasers in 1994 by BellSouth under the name Simon Personal Communicator. As well as setting and accepting cell calls, the touchscreen-prepared Simon could send and get faxes and messages. It incorporated a location book, schedule, arrangement scheduler, mini-computer, world time clock, and scratch pad, just as other visionary versatile applications like guides, stock reports and news.

The IBM Simon was produced by Mitsubishi Electric, which incorporated highlights from its own remote individual advanced right hand (PDA) and cell radio advances. It included a fluid precious stone presentation (LCD) and PC Card support. The Simon was monetarily fruitless, especially because of its cumbersome structure factor and restricted battery life, utilizing NiCad batteries instead of nickel-metal hydride batteries utilized in cell phones during the 90s lithium-particle batteries utilized in present day cell phones. The expression "cell phone" was not instituted until a year after the presentation of the Simon, showing up on paper as ahead of schedule as 1995, depicting AT&T's Phone Writer Communicator The expression "cell phone" was first utilized by Ericsson in 1997 to portray another gadget idea, the GS88.

Starting in the mid-late 90s, numerous individuals who had cell phones conveyed a different committed PDA gadget, running early forms of working frameworks like Palm OS, Newton OS, Symbian or Windows CE/Pocket PC. These working frameworks would later advance into early versatile working frameworks. In this period, the vast majority of the "cell phones" were crossover gadgets that consolidated these current comfortable PDA OS with the fundamental telephone equipment. The outcomes were gadgets that were bulkier than either devoted cell phones or PDAs yet permitted a restricted measure of cell Internet access. PDA and cell phone producers contended to lessening the size of gadgets. The main part of these cell phones, joined with their significant expense and costly information plans, in addition to different downsides like development impediments and diminished battery life contrasted with discrete independent gadgets, by and large, restricted their prevalence to "early adopters" and business clients who required convenient availability.

In March 1996, Hewlett-Packard delivered the OmniGo 700LX, an altered HP 200LX palmtop PC with a Nokia 2110 cell phone piggybacked onto it and ROM-based programming to help it. It had a 640×200 goal CGA viable four-conceal dark scale LCD screen and could be utilized to put and get calls and to make and get instant messages, messages and faxes. It was likewise 100% DOS 5.0 viable, permitting it to run a huge number of existing programming titles, including early forms of Windows.

In August 1996, Nokia delivered the Nokia 9000 Communicator, an advanced cell PDA dependent on the Nokia 2110 with a coordinated framework dependent on the PEN/GEOS 3.0 working framework from Geoworks. The two segments were joined by a pivot in what got known as a clamshell plan, with the showcase above and an actual QWERTY console underneath. The PDA gave email; schedule, address book, number cruncher and note pad applications; text-based Web perusing; and could send and get faxes. At the point when shut, the gadget could be utilized as a computerized cell phone.

Early smartphones
Telephones that utilized any critical information availability were as yet uncommon in external Japan until the presentation of the Danger Hiptop in 2002, which saw moderate accomplishment among U.S. customers as the T-Mobile Sidekick. Afterward, during the 2000s, business clients in the U.S. began to embrace gadgets dependent on Microsoft's Windows Mobile and BlackBerry cell phones from Research In Motion. American clients promoted the expression "Break Berry" in 2006 because of BlackBerry's habit-forming nature. In the U.S., the significant expense of information plans and relative uncommonness of gadgets with Wi-Fi capacities that could stay away from cell information network utilization kept the selection of cell phones principally to business experts and "early adopters."

Outside the U.S. furthermore, Japan, Nokia was seeing a good outcome with its cell phones dependent on Symbian, initially created by Psion for their coordinators, and it was the most mainstream cell phone OS in Europe during the center late 2000s. At first, Nokia's Symbian cell phones were centered around business with the" E arrangement," like Windows Mobile and BlackBerry gadgets at that point. From 2006 onwards, Nokia began creating shopper-centered cell phones, advocated by the diversion centered" N arrangement." Until 2010, Symbian was the world's most generally utilized cell phone working framework.

The touchscreen individual advanced partner (PDA)- inferred nature of adjusted working frameworks like Palm OS, the "Pocket PC" variants of what was later Windows Mobile, and the UIQ interface that was initially intended for pen-put together PDAs with respect to Symbian OS gadgets brought about some early cell phones having pointer based interfaces. These took into account virtual consoles and penmanship input, hence permitting a simple section of Asian characters.

By the mid-2000s, most of cell phones had an actual QWERTY console. Most utilized a "console bar" structure factor, similar to the BlackBerry line, Windows Mobile cell phones, Palm Treos, and a portion of the Nokia Eseries. A couple shrouded their full actual QWERTY console in a sliding structure factor, similar to the Danger Hiptop line. Some even had just a numeric keypad utilizing T9 text input, similar to the Nokia Nseries and different models in the Nokia Eseries. Resistive touchscreens with pointer based interfaces could, in any case, be found on a couple of cell phones, similar to the Palm Treos, which had dropped their penmanship contribution after a couple of early models that were accessible in forms with Graffiti rather than a console.

The last part of the 2000s and mid 2010s saw a change in cell phone interfaces from gadgets with actual consoles and keypads to ones with huge finger-worked capacitive touchscreens. The primary telephone of any sort with a huge capacitive touchscreen was the LG Prada, declared by LG in December 2006. This elegant component telephone was made in a joint effort with Italian extravagance architect Prada with a 3" 240x400 pixel screen.

In January 2007, Apple Computer presented the iPhone. It had a 3.5" capacitive touchscreen with twice the regular goal of most cell phone screens at that point and acquainted multi-contact with telephones, which permitted signals, for example, "squeezing" to zoom in or out on photographs, guides, and site pages. The iPhone was outstanding similar to the principal gadget of its sort focused at the mass market to desert the utilization of a pointer, console, or keypad normal of contemporary cell phones, all things being equal, utilizing an enormous touchscreen for direct finger contribution as its primary methods for the association.

The iPhone's working framework was additionally a shift away from past ones that were adjusted from PDAs and cell phones, to one incredible enough to try not to utilize a restricted, stripped-down internet browser requiring pages extraordinarily organized utilizing advances, for example, WML, HTML, or XHTML that past telephones upheld and rather run a rendition of Apple's Safari program that could without much of a stretch render full sites not explicitly intended for telephones.

Later, Apple transported a product update that gave the iPhone an inherent on-gadget App Store permitting direct remote downloads of outsider programming. This sort of concentrated App Store and free engineer apparatuses immediately turned into the new fundamental worldview for all cell phone stages for programming advancement, appropriation, disclosure, establishment, and installment, instead of costly designer instruments that necessary authority endorsement to utilize and reliance on outsider sources giving applications to different stages.

The benefits of a plan with programming adequately amazing to help progressed applications and a huge capacitive touchscreen influenced the advancement of another cell phone OS stage, Android, with a more BlackBerry-like model gadget rejected for a touchscreen gadget with a slide-out actual console, as Google's architects suspected at the time that a touchscreen couldn't totally supplant a real console and fastens. Android is based around an altered Linux part, again giving more force than versatile working frameworks adjusted from PDAs and highlight telephones. The primary Android gadget, the level sliding HTC Dream, was delivered in September 2008.

In 2012, Asus began exploring different avenues regarding a convertible docking framework named PadFone. The independent handset can be embedded into a tablet-sized screen unit with a strong coordinated battery and utilized all things considered.

In 2013 and 2014, Samsung explored different avenues regarding the cross breed blend of a minimized camera and cell phone, delivering the Galaxy S4 Zoom and K Zoom, each outfitted with coordinated 10× optical long range focal point and manual boundary settings (counting manual openness and center) a long time before these were broadly adjusted among cell phones. The S4 Zoom also has a turning handle ring around the focal point and a stand mount.

Chapter 3: Comparing between devices

When it comes to mobile devices —also known as a phone — you sure will get to see all kinds of terms. Terms such as 'Smartphone' and 'mobile phone' forms 2 frequently-used terms when it comes to movie devices. Yet, we also have the Tablet and smart watches. Now the question is, what's the disparity between these devices? Is there really any difference? Anyway, we will drive into them in this chapter and understand that fully well. We'll focus more on the Comparison between a mobile device and an intelligent device, and a mobile device is just a GSM, whereas a smart device includes Smart Android phones, smart Apple Phones, Tablets, iPads and smart watches. So let's start off.

- In making calls, both the mobile device and the smart device make calls, they have network properties.
- Both of these devices — the smart device and the mobile device- can send messages and receive messages.
- Actually in surfing the Internet, it is only sleeping devices that have that capacity to engagement into cellular network and internet services, a typical mobile phone cannot browse.
- In downloading applications, mobile devices only make use of those games, applications and platforms or installed in them. Oh the other hand, because smart devices have internet capabilities and can install any new application which is needed.
- Also, the keyboard or keypad or button of Mobile phones are usually physical, whereas the Keyboard of a smart device is usually virtual.
- Mobile phones sometimes have a camera installed in it's hardware. Still, the Camera is usually of low quality, or it can boil down to an average quality if fee times if it is ever present. Still, for smart devices, they always have a Camera that ranges from average to a very high or good camera.

What is a smartphone

Although we normally refer to smartphones as mobile phones, but most importantly, the 2 terms do refer technically to different devices. Both a mobile phone and a smartphone are mobile devices you can actually make use of to call and send text messages. And that actually is the place where a mobile phone stops, together with its functionality. Also, although some also feature a camera which forms part of our hard water during its compilation, a smartphone, on the other hand, has all kinds of extra functionalities, which may include Internet access, together with the very option of downloading applications and games from is store, as well as a camera — It usually has a bright and beautiful camera, and most often, it is better than the camera –web cam – of a PC. This then gives you the very option of answering calls and attending to emails using your phone. It also enables you to share photos in which you have taken with your camera together with your friends, and you can do that as fast as possible right away. Another difference is just that mobile phones most often have a physical keyboard, whereas on the other hand, a smartphone keyboard is usually virtual.

What is a cell phone

An adequate comparison between a smartphone and a mobile phone will call to mind that a smartphone has more options, although it is true that this doesn't necessarily mean it is preferable to a mobile phone. Your optional choice will have to determine which of the phone types is the better option for you. Actually, it may be that you are looking for a phone that is straight to the point to be use for calls and for sending text messages, but you do not actually need all those extra functions that comes with a smart phone. The way a mobile phone is so straight to the point can actually be very useful, it will just be like saying that the physical keyboard is friendly to be used by you. In fact, there will be no differences to it and interruptions such as well be seen in a smart phone in which the background applications can slow down the speed and the user experience of your device, or even pop up a particular thing like an Ad or advert and disturb you. But if you really want to get to the Internet or make downloads of certain applications and even take pictures, you will likely prefer a smartphone.

The Difference in Smartphones And Cellphones

There was a certain time — Although not too long ago — when several people make adequate use of a mobile phone, primarily those manufactured by companies such as Nokia, Sony Ericsson, or even Motorola and some other ones. Although it is true that phones from these manufacturing companies are still readily available in these days, although Sony Ericsson phones are excluded since they are now replaced by Sony phones, but we do have a lot more choices to make. There are new leading companies in the market now and there are some of the new categories they have, including the iPhones, then the Android devices, the Window devices, amongst others. Is it shocking to you and sometimes you wonder how all these things changed? Well, it is for us to know firstly, let us get some of these terms right.

Actually, Mobile phones as well as Cellphones are just the very same thing; the mobile phone as a name is just a term that is very akin in the British world, it is so common in the UK and all Europe, on the other hand, the cellphone is yet another term but the same name with the cell phone, it is a term that is more common and popularly used and known in regions of the US. The smartphone is another type of mobile phone and it is even the simpler phones that were so generally over the past decade ago and are now called feature phones. So, in other words, both the term — smartphones — and the other term — feature phones — can be used to either name mobile phones or cellphones.

So far, since we have clarified the various terms, and we can understand them, let us then drive into the actual details at once. Okay, before the launch of the recent 4G networks, a very few enhancements just like the High-Speed Packet Access — also represented with the acronym; HSPA — were fully included in the mobile networks which made an improvement to the mobile data or the internet quality of the devices in a very considerable way. Now, just as mobile internet became more common in this time, it become so much possible for us to browse the web and stream videos — make life steaming — in very high quality, and that can be done directly from our mobile devices — isn't it awesome? Our demand for 'being connected' then improved, so many people started making use of mobile phones for their online communication even in getting and sending mails through email. Then in the year 2007, just with the launch of the newly manufactured iPhone, the industry was transformed tremendously in favour of mobile devices that offers people the opportunity to do more activities online than just making voice calls and Sending text messages through SMS. Those mobile phones that are like a computer, in which most of us make use in this present time, are actually called "smartphones."

Therefore, smartphones are then the advanced form of these mobile devices, or you can say that smart phones are actually cellphones that have computer-like functionalities and capabilities in addition to the very basic features that cell phones have. These phones allow you the opportunity to do a lot of things, the chance to get most of your online work done, online jobs such as web browsing, or the use of online applications and gaming frame wares, or even watching videos, etcetera. The very basic phone features, just like making voice calls and Sending text messages using SMS, are also very much included. So, whereas the other simpler phones will just allow you to make voice calls, and send text messages using the SMS Applications messaging platform, any device that allows you and grants you the access to do some basic online services are called 'feature phones.'

Now, just the same way as computers, these phones and devices have a microprocessor installed into them, it also has RAM, internal phone storage, and external storage that may be an SD card an OTG. All these smartphones have web browsers and many vast number of mobile applications that are easily available from the app marketplace, which is popularly known and referred to as app stores — an example of these mobile market places includes the Android play store Apple Store and others. These mobile Applications possess the due capacity to use device functionalities and frame wares and computing power to perform several tasks, just like a computer can do by using the software installed in it. Many applications that certain business ventures make use of business applications and security applications can also run on these phones. Smartphones are really common in this our time, and there are many phone manufacturers out there. And as a result of that, the prices for smartphones may vary considerably Completely l also.

Almost every one of the smartphones there has capabilities that support touch-screen. Smartphone users can easily make and receive regular voice calls and send and also get instant messages (SMS). What's more, the clients can likewise get to cutting edge applications and peruse the web actually like they can do on a PC. Through the use of several specific applications, smartphones make it very easy for users to gain access to internet-based voice calling and even messaging services such as Messenger and WhatsApp. Email and satellite route are among different administrations that cell phones empower in a simple to utilize way.

How Do Smartphones Work?

Like any other year of any mobile phone, smartphone users require a connection that can be gotten from an operator is a mobile device or a provider is any service. Once the service is enabled, either via a plastic SIM or an eSIM, the smartphone can connect to the network of his mobile device and be able to get access to all other services which may have phone calls inclusive to it, as well as text messages, and the internet too. The traditional voice calls that are a general note to every mobile device typically take place on the very part of the mobile network short-circuited. Smartphones can use many technologies to get access to the web service.

The packet part of the 2G and the 3G and the 4G networks that have been switched is the very important way of using the internet services, yes, it is also very possible for one to connect to a WiFi network. Most of the smartphones of these days Comes with it an embedded GPS capability — short term for Global Positioning System — which enables satellite navigation for the users. These phones also possess specific applications that can be used for email services, even with the capacity to send message pop-ups to the clients to know when they receive emails.

Based on the manufacturing company of your phone, you may need to have different mobile operating systems (OS). Now, the two very prominent operating systems are the Android Operating System and iOS that make up for the majority of the mobile OS market share. Other operating systems are one of the technologies below Windows, Series 40, and Symbian and Blackberry. iOS is from Apple for iPhones, whereas Android is from Google and used by some manufacturers including Google themselves (Google Pixel), then you have Samsung, then Huawei, and Honor and a few others. The mobile applications for any operating systems can be downloaded directly from their respective app stores.

About Featured Phones

Although smartphones are the common devices at this time, people choose to use simpler mobile phones, actually known as feature phones. Feature phones gives you basic phone features together with very restricted web-based services. A feature phone user can actually make and receive phone calls and then send/receive text messages. A feature phone also has a couple of fundamental underlying versatile applications and a portable internet browser. Every one of the portable applications is introduced on the component telephones straight by the producer of the device, and the users of any feature phone are not required to download or even install any form of applications, not even 1. Any feature phone user will have a need of mobile service from a network operator or service provider.

Once the service is not enabled, the feature phone can then connect to the mobile network and make adequate use its services in order to make and receive phone calls, and be able to send and also receive text messages through the use of the part of the mobile network which has been circuit-switched. And now especially, it can also use the packet-switched part of the network to make use of any of the internet-enabled applications and mobile web browser especially. Some component telephones additionally have WiFi ability which permits them to interface with any other fixed wireless internet.

Chapter 4: Comparing Between Operating Systems

Android is a mobile operating system(OS) in view of an altered form of the Linux bit and other open-source programming, planned principally for touchscreen cell phones, for example, cell phones and tablets. Android is created by a consortium of engineers known as the Open Handset Alliance and financially supported by Google. It was uncovered in November 2007, with the primary business Android gadget, the HTC Dream, being dispatched in September 2008.

It is free and open-source programming; its source code is known as Android Open Source Project (AOSP), which is principally authorized under the Apache License. In any case, most Android gadgets transport with extra restrictive programming pre-introduced, most strikingly Google Mobile Services (GMS) which incorporates center applications like Google Chrome, the computerized conveyance stage Google Play and the related Google Play Services improvement stage.

About 71percent of Android cell phones run Google's environment; contending Android biological systems and forks incorporate Fire OS (created by Amazon) or LineageOS. Nonetheless, the "Android" name and logo are brand names of Google which force norms to limit "uncertified" gadgets outside their environment to utilize Android marking.

The source code has been utilized to foster Android variations on a scope of other gadgets, like game control center, advanced cameras, compact media players, PCs and others, each with a particular UI. All things considered, realized subordinates incorporate Android TV for TVs and Wear OS for wearables, both created by Google. Programming bundles on Android, which utilize the APK design, are for the most part conveyed through exclusive application stores like Google Play Store, Samsung Galaxy Store, Huawei AppGallery, Cafe Bazaar, and GetJar or open-source stages like Aptoide or F-Droid.

Android Inc. was established in Palo Alto, California, in October 2003 by Andy Rubin, Rich Miner, Nick Sears, and Chris White. Rubin portrayed the Android project as having "gigantic potential in creating more astute cell phones that are more mindful of its proprietor's area and inclinations." The early expectations of the organization were to foster a high-level working framework for computerized cameras, which was the premise of its contribution to financial backers in April 2004. At that point, the organization concluded that the market for cameras was not enormous enough for its objectives. After five months, it redirected its endeavors and pitched Android as a handset working framework that would equal Symbian and Microsoft Windows Mobile.

Rubin experienced issues drawing in financial backers right off the bat, and Android was confronting expulsion from its office space. Steve Perlman, a dear companion of Rubin, brought him $10,000 in real money in an envelope and presently wired an undisclosed sum as seed financing. Perlman declined a stake in the organization and has expressed, "I did it since I put stock in the thing, and I needed to help Andy."

In July 2005, Google procured Android Inc. for in any event, $50 million. Its key workers, including Rubin, Miner, Sears, and White, joined Google to obtain. Very little was thought about the clandestine Android Inc. at that point, with the organization having given not many subtleties other than that it was making programming for cell phones. At Google, the group drove by Rubin fostered a cell phone stage fueled by the Linux piece. Google advertised the stage to handset producers and transporters on the guarantee of giving an adaptable, upgradeable framework. Google had "arranged a progression of equipment segments and programming accomplices and motioned to transporters that it was available to different levels of participation."

Hypothesis about Google's aim to enter the versatile interchanges market kept on working through December 2006. An early model had a nearby likeness to a BlackBerry telephone, with no touchscreen and an actual QWERTY console, however, the appearance of 2007's Apple iPhone implied that Android "needed to return to the planning phase." Google later changed its Android determination reports to express that "Touchscreens will be upheld," albeit "the Product was planned with the presence of actual discrete catches as a supposition, accordingly a touchscreen can't totally supplant actual catches." By 2008, both Nokia and BlackBerry declared touch-based cell phones to match the iPhone 3G, and Android's concentrate in the long run changed to simply touchscreens. The first economically accessible cell phone running

Android was the HTC Dream, otherwise called T-Mobile G1, reported on September 23, 2008.

Since 2008, Android has seen various updates which have steadily improved the working framework, adding new highlights and fixing bugs in past discharges. Each significant delivery is named in sequential request after a sweet or sweet treat, with the initial not many Android variants being classified "Cupcake," "Donut," "Eclair," "Froyo," and "Jellybean" in a specific order. During its declaration of Android KitKat in 2013, Google clarified that "Since these gadgets make our lives so sweet, every Android variant is named after a treat," albeit a Google representative told CNN in a meeting that "It's similar to an inner group thing, and we like to be a tad how could I say somewhat questionable in the matter, I'll say."

In 2010, Google dispatched its Nexus arrangement of gadgets, a setup where Google joined forces with various gadget makers to create new gadgets and present new Android forms. The arrangement was portrayed as having "assumed a significant part in Android's set of experiences by presenting new programming emphasess and equipment guidelines no matter how you look at it" and got known for its "bulge free" programming with "opportune ... refreshes". At its engineer gathering in May 2013, Google reported an extraordinary variant of the Samsung Galaxy S4. Rather than utilizing Samsung's possesses Android customization, the telephone runs on "stock Android" and was guaranteed to get new framework refreshes quickly. The gadget would turn into the beginning of the Google Play release program and be trailed by different gadgets, including the HTC One Google Play version and Moto G Google Play version. In 2015, Ars Technica composed that "Recently, the remainder of the Google Play version Android telephones in Google's online retail facade were recorded as "not, at this point ready to move" and that "Presently they're gone, and it looks a ton like a program has wrapped up."

Features of an Andriod Device
Status Bar

Along with the highest point of the screen is a status bar, showing data about the gadget and its availability. This status bar can be pulled (swiped) down here to uncover a notice screen where applications show significant data or updates, just as fast admittance to framework controls and switches, for example, show brilliance, network settings (WiFi, Bluetooth, Mobile information), sound mode, and spotlight. Merchants may carry out broadened settings like the capacity to change the spotlight splendor.

Home Screen

Android gadgets boot to the home screen, the essential route and data "center point" on Android gadgets, comparable to the work area found on PCs. Android home screens are commonly comprised of application symbols and gadgets; application symbols dispatch the related application, though gadgets show live, auto-refreshing substance, for example, a climate figure, the client's email inbox, or the news ticker straightforwardly on the home screen. A home screen might be comprised of a few pages, between which the client can swipe to and fro. Outsider applications accessible on Google Play and other application stores can broadly re-subject the home screen and surprisingly impersonate the vibe of other working frameworks, like Windows Phone. Most producers tweak the look and highlights of their Android gadgets to separate themselves from their rivals.

Notifications

These are "short, opportune, and pertinent data about your application when it's not being used." When tapped, clients are coordinated to a screen inside the application identifying with the warning. Starting with Android 4.1, "Jam Bean," "expandable notices" permit the client to tap a symbol on the warning for it to extend and show more data and conceivable application activities directly from the notice.

Application List

An "All Apps" screen records all introduced applications, with the capacity for clients to drag an application from the rundown onto the home screen. A new screen allows clients to switch between as of late utilized applications.

The rundown may seem next to each other or covering, contingent upon the Android variant.

Charging when powered off

While associating or disengaging charging power and when in the blink of an eye inciting the force catch or home catch, all while the gadget is controlled off, a visual battery meter whose appearance shifts among sellers shows up on the screen, permitting the client to rapidly evaluate the charge status of a fueled off without booting it up first. Some showcase the battery rate.

Memory Management

Since Android gadgets are normally battery-fueled, Android is intended to oversee cycles to keep power utilization at least. At the point when an application isn't being used, the framework suspends its activity so that, while accessible for sure fire use as opposed to shut, it doesn't utilize battery force or CPU assets. Android deals with the applications put away in memory naturally: when memory is low, the framework will start imperceptibly and consequently shutting idle cycles, beginning with those that have been dormant for the longest measure of time.

Accessible For Users

Andriod offers so many features for their users, these features include a voice command, voice reading, gesture command e.t.c these features helps the users access and enjoy the android device.

Security

Andriod comes with strong security for the Andriod device. This helps to keep the device safe and stop hackers from penetrating the device. Security such as; Passcodes, Face IDs, Pins are required before you can unlock the device.

Chapter 5: Managing your Mobile Phone

In this topic, we'll see how to use a cell phone. See, from flip phones even down to camera phones and all the way to a phones with applications which support the playing of music and other multimedia, cell phones are a very great help to us in making communications, and it fully connects us to the world in a simpler and straight forward way. Now especially, they are a must for teenagers and adults alike, and often times, it is essential to acquire it for work, or school, and in order for us to socialize more. So let's start our discussion with the technicalities of finding a good cell phone for your use.

Finding the Best Cell Phone Plan

The first thing for you to do is to make a research of local cell phone carriers who are in your area, or the popular phone and mobile devices which are common in your country. Although it depends on the region you're living in, there will be so many phone companies with a wide variety of plans here and there. You can also decide to go on the various website of these devices to know more about them and their mobile phone plan or else, you can also make a visit to their shops and ask them for a brief information about their various services. Yet another way to get prepared to acquire a new cell phone they will serve you better is for you to read reviews and be able to ask others what their experiences of using each brand of a cell phone are, how they related with their provider, which version and model of the phone are best, and which one will serve you better. In real fact, the number of people making use of a certain provider is a very good marker of what carrier best works in your very area.

You need to seek a provider with the best network coverage that can support your area and country. A good company should readily make provisions of a truly large range of mobile or network coverage and reception that is truly reliable. This then will mean that they will own the most number of cellular towers and network stations in order for them to provide network service to more even more wider areas. It gives an assurance that all your calls and any of the communications you make won't be dropped down while you're moving down from one place to another and you will also be very able to make reception of service in even very low populated regions or underground locations.

In fact, many of the countries will have a unique map of every cellular tower that makes a label of which towers are used by which provider that you can actually find by doing a very quick internet search. A very good provider should have the most towers in the area or areas where you are living it or where you are most often, where you visit frequently. A company may make advertisement of their plans, which actually come with great deals, but this does not necessarily mean that they will have a very reliable network. A very great plan is only useful if you can carry out calls and reception services wherever you may be. If you are actually the type that travels a lot, you need to consider looking for a carrier that provides national or even international coverage.

Then, the very next thing you must need to do is for you to evaluate the network speeds of the data of your cell phone providers, such as network coverage, as well as data coverage as it depends on your region and the carrier too. Data is very useful if you plan to use the Internet on your phone or if you have actually had a smartphone. You need to make certain comparisons about the speed of the data network and the various carriers' speeds. You can and will always find this very notification on their website or from a close sales representative. One more thing to note is that the higher the number of kilobits per second (kbps), the faster you will actually be able to use the internet to upload and download data. Actually, technology is always updating and upgrading with time. The very latest data "G" of mobile technology will be the fastest, and this "G" actually stands for generation. There are several generations of mobile network, and in these days, we are right between 4G and 5G. However, not every mobile phone or device can support our time's latest and fastest data connection.

You then can make a decision about what cellular service plan is right for you. The very plan you will choose will truly dictate which kind of phone you can ever get — either directly or indirectly — what you can actually do with your Mobile phone, or the length of time you will have to stay with the carrier, and even how much you will every have to pay a single month. You then need to choose a plan that is really within your budget but will at the very same time still allow you to have the best features you've ever wanted to use on your phone. Some of these common but really important features include the following:-

- **Call Minutes:** You talk about how many call times per minute you are being offered monthly. Then the amount of money which it may cost for you to go over to the very maximum of the same. Then you need also to know if the minutes you could use rollover to the next month since you didn't use it. In fact, some of the providers will designate certain times of the day or some of the days in a week where you really can use an unlimited amount of minutes to make and receive calls. Some may even offer unlimited calling.
- **Text Messaging:** In your time, texting — text message — is probably the most important must-have feature of cell phones. And most providers will really offer unlimited texting or a certain number of free texts. So you should be extremely careful about it, some of the providers may have to charge you just for opening texts.
- **Data Usage:** Network providers will have to offer varying amounts of data you can use each month to download and upload from the Internet. This actually can range anywhere from 500 MB at the minimum range to 6 GB at the maximum range, even down to an unlimited amount of data usage.
- **Voicemail:** Of course, there is usually an additional charge for someone to be able to use this given feature. It is so very essential any useful too when you can not always answer your cell phone. However, in calling your voicemail box, this may count towards using up call time minutes.

- **Caller ID:** Caller ID is a very crucial technology in our world today. Most of the plans will include caller ID now, and it is a highly demanded and expected feature.
- **Contracts:** Most of the network plans do necessarily require you to sign a 1 - 3 year contract with your provider. This is usually because you will duly receive a price that has discounts just for the cost of the physical phone, even right up front or a way to finance your phone throughout your contract. However, you will still be making the payments of the very cost implications of the plan that comes with the phone's contract and any fees that serve as additional features and even taxes.
- **Family Plans:** If it happens to be that so many family members make use of cell phones, it may then be even more affordable for users to go with a family plan. The number of
- minutes, and data, and even texts are shared among your family to use each month.

Purchase a pre-paid phone plan. Assuming you do have bad credit, and you want a specific way to save money, or you are simply seeking to try out a cell phone even without signing up for a long contract, all you may just want a prepaid or even a pay as you go plan. Howbeit, some of the cons there are includes:-

- Phones of all types cost full price and you must have to pay for it all at once. But, some of the previous models of phones which are really old phones, are relatively cheap.
- Your network coverage is not the carrier's top priority. In fact, even though you may opt for a carrier that has the very best coverage in your area, you also may need to contract providers who will have top priority when it comes over to their network.
- Customer service sometimes may be lacking.

Choosing the Right Phone

If you notice that your cellular needs are so simple, you will have to choose a classic mobile phone. It may be that what you wish to do is just that you just want to connect to your friends and family through a phone call or a text message. Mobile phones are specially designed for ease of use, in addition, it also comes in a variety of models which may include the flip-phone design or it can also come as a slide out keyboard. The cost price of any classic mobile phone is so much lower when compared to other devices.

Some of the contracts will even grant the phone for free. Look, classic mobile phones are quite durable. This promises to be so great if your life involves being in certain situations where you may drop your telephone or need to utilize it in shaky circumstances. You will not need to stress over breaking them as effectively as a cell phone. If you are an older person and want a very simple wireless phone, classic mobile phones will show you the best choice. Some phones have enlarged keypads which forms part of their frame were to be used for easy dialing.

You can actually invest into a smartphone. Smartphones can just be referred to as mini-computers and they are actually the very most popular choice of phone for consumers. They have touch screens, they also have connectivity for wifi connection. They are also a story made for HD cameras. They also come in different operating systems (OS) and different sizes.

- **Android Of Google:** Let's see another Operating System there is, this next one is actually the Android Operating system developed and maintained by Google. Android as an Operating System grants us the offer of more advanced flexibility for developers — for those who want to customize and set up the very way in which their Operating System appears and functions. This Operating System is very highly customizable if you can only know the actual basics of Technical Education. It is so useful if you would love to develop an application, especially if you want to dinner right into application development.

- **Windows Of Microsoft:** As a business owner, this Operating System should really be right for you — it is greatly essential in the business world. Windows have integrated into it so many of the traditional Windows applications, including Microsoft Office — almost all the software in this series, Microsoft Exchange, and even Microsoft's cloud platform — isn't that awesome. Microsoft's windows Operating System offers users so much more power to create and customize any advanced documents.

- **iOS of Apple:** iOS is the mobile operating system that Apple uses for its iPhones. iOS was first released back in 2007 and its main rival is Google's Android. Thanks to this operating system, many functions used today have become popular, such as the zoom in and out and the swipe gesture. A peculiarity of iOS is the abandonment of the physical Home button. Additionally, deeper integration with Apple apps such as Apple Music, Podcast, TV and more can be seen. Apple has been known for supporting its devices for many years with regular updates, from bug fixes and security issues to great releases that offer exciting new features.

You can also consider alternative phones and devices, devices such as tablets or personal digital assistants (PDA). Personal digital assistants (PDAs) are not very popular in these recent times, although there are some of the upgraded models of these devices, some of which includes; the Blackberry phone, which work so very well if your attention is fundamentally on perusing the Internet without every one of the additional highlights that accompany cell phones. Tablets have bigger screens and have greater flexibility and force near a work area or PC, yet have the accommodation of a cell phone.

Making Adequate Use Of Your Cell Phone

With your Mobile phone, you can actually create a contact list, this week enable you to call anytime just by a single click, rather than going through the whole process of putting in a particular pine number of 10, 11, or 12 digits, and sometimes while doing that, mistakes are inevitable. So, you can actually create a contact list step by step by simply gathering up the various phone numbers of the people who you want to talk to either often or in the future. As for smartphones, there will usually be an application or a specific icon or service with a phone picture. You just need to Tap on this application or icon for you to view your contacts. You can also click the button to add any new contact of your choice, and this is usually indicated by a symbol, it usually is indicated by a "+" symbol.

All you just have to do here is for you to put in the whole detailed information of your contact as much as can be allowed and not especially, the phone number of the person, and this you can do with the keypad of the Greene waste of you mobile phone. As soon as you do this, you can then save it by clicking on the "save" button. If you don't have a safe button on your phone, you can then see a symbol of a ticked good, click on it and there you are, you contact is saved. If you are making use of a classic phone, then it is as easy as just dialing the number and then pressing a button that could then allow you to create a new l brand new contact.

Mobile devices tend to have different tabs for you to keep your favorite numbers, as well as the recent calls you've made, and the contacts also, keypad, and voicemail too. It is also good to go ahead and read the operating manual of your device since there is much disparity between each Operating System, they can vary slightly even in the place of their different contacts and the way they are made. For instance, Android phones will differ so widely from iPhones and even Windows phones and operating systems.

Making calls adequately

You then can make calls by choosing or by dialing any number at all, and as you dial the number, you then need to press the "send" button or the "call" button. This button is often colored with green color with certain letters or symbols. Then, you need to proceed as with any other phone call. As soon as your done making the call, you can end the call by pressing the "end" button, which is indicated with a red color and some letters or symbols. Also, the calls you make will usually end automatically as soon as the person you spoke to hangs up his or her own phone, although it is best for you to get right into the habit of hanging up your phone yourself as soon as your done talking, due to the fact that cells are billed mainly by call minute.

Looking at missed calls

You can also look at any missed calls or even recent calls within the phone app on a smartphone like Android, or you can choose to go through your menu on a classic phone in order for you to get access to it. There are also details such as knowing about the person who the call came in from, then you can also know when the call was made and took up options to redial and save new contacts, which is also available.

Setting up your voicemail box

Most of the phones which are available will usually have a button that dials your voicemail box directly for you when the need arises. If you can't find this button, then it's not a big deal, holding unto "1" on your keypad will automatically dial your voicemail number. You then need to follow the promptings that appear with the system for you to create your own very password, then you need to record your name announcement too and make a record of your greeting. If you may not like to record your own greeting, the system will use its own programmed greeting and customize it using the name you have recorded earlier. You then can change your password, or your name, or even the greeting anytime you wish, and this you can do by just dialing the number of your choice mail, and as soon as you do, you just need to follow the menu prompts they or presents with it. Then, when you receive a voicemail, then your smartphone will alert you or pop up a notification on your display notification panel. So tap the voicemail number or hold "1" to access your mailbox and get started. You then need to Input your password and pay close attention to your messages. Then you need to follow the prompts that will appear for you to either callback the number, or save the message or even delete the message.

Messaging your contacts:

Most of the mobile phones will tag your text messaging application as "Messages," or it can even tag it as "Messaging." You then have to "Create a New Message" in that place by clicking on the create new message button or the "+" icon. On the other hand, you can decide to choose a contact directly from your contact list, and as you have, you need to press the options key and look out for an option that will allow you to send a message to that very contact.

If what you have is a classic phone that does not have the QWERTY keyboards, then if may require you to learn and use the T9 keyboard or predictive text, depending on your mobile phone support. Smartphones will have an array of serial messaging apps you can download and make use of. Some of the messaging applications will make use of the cellular network of your provider in order for you to send messages.

Locking your Device :

Locking the keyboard of your mobile phone or the screen of your smartphone will help to secure it from pocket dials, accidental presses or thefts. Each mobile device and Operating System will have a different way of locking its keypad. Android smartphones will only require you to enter a definite password or a number of 4-digit as a code. You can check through your settings or you can look through the user manual for you to get to know how to lock your phone.

Most of the classic phones there are have their keypad locked. This is not actually a form of security rather, it is a preventive measure rich is there to act against pocket dialing. If you have a mobile flip phone, this should not be of much worry to you. If not, most phones get locked by pressing the menu key, which is quickly followed by the asterisks key. In order to unlock your device after that, all you have to do is for you to press the unlock key which is shown on the key of your phone, and as you do that, you then press the asterisk key with it in order to unlock the device.

On the other hand, if you are very worried about theft, most smartphones have certain apps which are also used to find where you are located as you are with your phone, or if it is stolen, you will be told where the person that stole your device is at every point in time.

Connecting to a WiFi network:

Most of the users of classic — or mobile _ phones have a problem connecting their device to a WiFi network. WiFi is important since your phone will no longer be using its routine data connection in don't internet services. Smartphones accept this feature very well. Smart phones like Android, when connected to a WiFi network, will stop using data connection. Therefore, you will no longer find their limitation to the amount of data your plan offers. Let's see how these things are done in various devices.

- **iPhones:** For this device, you need to go to the Settings icon and there press the Wi-Fi bar. Turn it on if it is not already on and choose a network from the list that is dropped down. You will then need to enter a password if you have a protected network that is locked with a key icon. Then, what you have to do is for you to Tap the "Join" button and you'll join.
- **Androids:** Of you're right on the home screen of your Android device, tap the Application icon and then open the Settings application. You should make sure the Wi-Fi master control is switched on in the top right hand corner and as soon as you do that, you then need to select an available network in the area where you live. Next, you will need to type the password in if the network is protected. Then you tap on the "Connect" button.
- **Windows:** As for windows phones, you need to swipe to the left of your screen to reveal your App List, then tap on the Settings and then on Wi-Fi. Ensure that the wifi is actually switched on and select a preferred network from the list of available networks in your area. There will be a need for you to enter a password if the network is protected. As soon as you go that, Tap on "Done."

As soon as you have been connected to a Wi-Fi network, you will see it's symbol appearing on the status bar — on the top Right or left corner — of your device. For most devices, it will replace the "G" data symbol to show you that it is no longer using the current data of your carrier.

Learn how to download apps. Most of the available smartphones will have a set of applications which are already downloaded into the device, one of them should be the application store of your operating system. You just need to Tap on the icon of this application and as it launches you into your application's environment, you have to search up the applications you wish to install for your work. You may be in need of setting up an account to help you better in downloading your apps. Your device should prompt you to set up an account, a new account that most often will need your personal information and even certain payment options.

iPhones make use of the App Store application and require any one who is a user to set up an Apple ID. Android devices, on the other hand, make use of the Google Play app store. Window devices make it's installations of the applications it uses from the Windows Store. Some of the applications cost some cash. So you need to ensure that you have correct payment information right down in your acc. So be careful whenever you are allowing other people to make use of your phone or your account to make downloads of your desired applications. In most cases, a password is usually needed to download any of the applications you need to install, which costs money to protect you from any unwanted purchases.

Some applications have in-app purchases and certain options for you to buy more of the features in order for you to upgrade the application you downloaded. Classic phones do not usually have the necessary application stores which you can download from. Some of the models that came out later of classic phones will have games, pictures, or even music applications.

Charging your Phone: You need to charge your phone regularly by plugging it to a light source with a charger. Mobile devices have a battery life indicator which is there to tell you the percentage left on the Battery of your phone to be filled or the time remaining of your battery life when it is discharging. In addition, most devices will warn you or remind you when its battery life is running low. Also, learn to Invest into different types of chargers for your phones such as a car charger, or dock chargers to be used in your house and for home audio systems, or even another extra charger.

Chapter 6: Managing your smartphone and Tablet

Android technology forms part of the most popular computing platform throughout the whole world, in a very large part, due to its open-source nature that is so so powerful and stunning. Several users around the world have a really appreciable love for Android as a device, and for the plethora of applications and several features that comes with it, and sleep because it is very very very customizable, on the other hand in some cases, it can all get confusing in a bit. Google is always making several and subsequent update, tweaks and new features, as well as stunning features in it's hard ware which makes it's use unique and just as user friendly as possible, and for it's user and devices like Samsung, Tecno and LG can add their very own stuff on top of that. It can actually be hard to keep up so well, so let's see how we can manage a smartphone — Basically android, then Tablets and iPhone.

Configure Your Lock Screen

Android as a smartphone offers a variety of secure lock screens. Most Android devices will prompt you to do this during the basic setup, as we saw earlier and you should. The very basic defaults are PIN code, then the pattern, and the password. In this age we're living in, most devices now can offer fingerprint security which probably is the very fastest way for any user to unlock his or her device. To control your lock screen, then you have to mine over to the system settings, and there find the Security menu. Some devices even have a different lock screen menu. This means that you will need to have a secure lock screen to use features that may include Android Pay and even the common factory reset protection.

Disabling Bloatware

Most mobile and smart phones come with some already pre-installed applications, and for some of them, you won't ever want to keep them around. Anyway, you are lucky enough to know that in these days, any pre-installed bloat can be adequately uninstalled by making use of the Play Store or by finding it right in the application settings menu. Anyways, anything that is part of the system image is non-removable. So what you can do is just for you to disable it by opening the application menu, which you can access from the main system settings. As soon as you finding the application in your list, then right at the very top, there will be a button labeled 'Disable' that eliminates it from your application cabinet and keeps it from running behind the scenes.

Finding Your Phone

All of us occasionally may in one way or the other gotten or devices missen, either we lost it by theft, accident or several other unforseen circumstances, but ee lost track of our phone. It may even be that it was hiding in the couch's cushions or lying somewhere on the kitchen counter. You don't north need to go crazy at all as you go round about looking for your phone; you just need to make use of the "Find my phone" tool developed by Google, which earlier was known as Android Device Manager. You can access this through the web, of you can get this on a mobile device or even on any computer like a PC. All you need do is just for your to just sign into your Google account and pick your missing telephone starting from the drop menu. The job of Google now is to reach out and shows you where your device is at every single point. You can also try to ring the phone, even if it is in silent mode, and you will get to see your device. Even if it is in a worse state, you can remotely erase the phone's data to protect your data.

Mobile Data Tracking

Data caps are akin across several mobile carriers, and the various rates of data just keep getting faster and faster. Thus to make sure that you don't blow through your month to month apportioning, visit the information use menu in the framework settings. A few telephones consider this something somewhat extraordinary, yet it's directly close to the top in every case. Here, you can set your arrangement reset date, make an admonition limit, and even have information consequently impaired when you're going to bring about an overage. Assuming that isn't what you like, be prepared guaranteed that Google has an application in the Play Store called Datally. Datally is an application that assists clients with gathering information directly from the settings menu, and it can restrict foundation information with a clever coasting counter to follow your information and data.

Do Not Disturb Settings

The notification settings of any android device are kind of confusing right now. Google has revamped it a few times in some of their recent updates. You will then have to find the settings for this very feature either in the popup of your volume control property when you click on it, you don't report the toggle or by going into the system settings for notifications, which usually can found inside the Sound and notification tab in the settings tab. It will be called Do Not Disturb for most devices. In this menu, you can choose when Not Disturb is switched on naturally, what is obstructed, and if any contacts are permitted to ring through at any rate. On the Pie gadgets, Do Not Disturb defaults likewise figure out how to conceal your notices also. Try to change that setting in the event that you actually need to perceive what's happening in the notification bar.

Digital Wellbeing

You may see yourself spending a whole lot of time on your phone sometimes, but Android has got some tools to help you avoid that. The Digital Wellbeing suite, which is available in Android form 9 and later shows you what applications you've been utilizing, for how long, and offers approaches to prevent that from occurring. The settings menu can really separate applications on a diagram and draw a course of events for applications you need to scale back. The outline tracks notices and opens too. There's likewise a "Wind down" mode that actually fades slowly on the screen in other to grayscale as bedtime approaches.

Back Up Photos

There's nothing so worse than losing or breaking a phone just for you to realize that your photos are not backed up in any way. You can avoid this by just opening the Google Photos application and following all the prompts that come with it by enabling auto-backup. The default mode is always the "high quality" and then the with unlimited space. You will have to packs your photographs, yet they look shockingly great. In the event that you need to save the first picture, you can select to utilize your Drive extra room. You get up to 15GB free and can even purchase more.

"OK Google" Voice Prompt

Google search is at the core of all Android telephones, and you can begin looking whenever just by saying, "Alright Google." This deals with the home screen and in the inquiry box; however, if you go into the hunt settings, you can get OK Google working all over. In the hunt settings, go to Voice > Voice Match. Simply turn on the "Entrance with Voice Match" alternative and the telephone will have you say "Alright Google" a couple of times to become familiar with your voice. Presently you can utilize the hot-word any time the gadget is alert from any screen. A few gadgets additionally support this when the screen is off, while others possibly work when the gadget is conscious.

Use of Google Assistant

Have your ever set up OK Google? If you have done so, then you have got two awesome ways to access Google Assistant. Therefore, to access Google Assistant, just use OK Google or long-press the home button. And as you do, just start talking. This feature was exclusive to the Pixel for a few months, but it rolled out to every Android phone running Marshmallow or higher. Google Assistant does understand more context and natural language than the very old voice of Google search feature. This can then be integrated with third-party services like IFTTT, Samsung Smart-Things, and Nest. It is so great at home automation and searching the web, and it can even read you the news of the day by detecting later need and yelling you about it.

Making use of your device's Screen Pinning

If you really need to hand over your device to someone else, but you don't want them to peep around your phone, going into other Applications, then it is a very easy task, you can make use of your device screen pinning. This is a straightforward way to do it — just pin the screen. You can enable this by default on most of the devices, but if it is not so, you need to check the security menu in your device settings and set it up there. Next, you need to Tap on the app icon on any Application in the multitasking interface and there, you can select the "Pin" option to prevent them from switching in between Applications on your dear phone. If you really do have a secure lock screen, you then can require that unlock method for you to leave the pinned app.

The use of Swipe Input on the Keyboard of your device.

Just always and frequently tapping the screen keyboard or your phone with your thumbs is okay as an input method, especially for beginners, but most phones and smart devices have specific swipe input built into them. You can try it out by just giving it a shot, just by dragging across the letters for each specific word. This swipe input's accuracy widely varies by various gadget, yet you can likewise introduce an alternate console that may suit you better. You can access the Gboard keyboard of Google, developed and maintained by them, yet there are myriads of other keyboard which have swipe properties included in them, some of which includes the SwitfKey with its plethora of settings as well as TouchPal keyboard.

Applying different power modes using the Power-Saving mode of your device

All Android devices possess a useful power-saving mode of certain types — it may either be two or sometimes three of them. Head to the battery menu, which is usually accessed in your device's Settings, and there you click on the Battery option. And that is how it is on most phones for you to see these settings for your power saving mode. For instance, Samsung offers us a regular power-saving mode that reduces the screen brightness and makes the device's CPU slower. Also then, there is yet an ultra power saver that fully locks the device to just a few essential applications by default. Finally, just like those from Google, most phones grant us an offer of basic power saving modes just like the former that can be switched on on their own when the device reaches at a particular battery level — let's say 30%. This is definitely something you should learn to set up.

System Dark Theme

Several other Applications — especially those developed and maintained by Google — do have bright white styles. Beginning from the recent Android 10, many system-wide dark themes can really toggle those Applications and parts of the system User Interface (UI) to a nice but muted black. It is really available in the Display settings or more conveniently right in the quick settings tab. Infected some devices also have those options to help schedule the dark theme so it automatically flips on every night and flips off early in the morning. Only those Applications that have been developed for the major aim of theming API will really work well, but that list is growing as the day enfolds.

Using your device Manager to Manage Default Applications

Several actions on an Android device will have to ask you to set up a default Application, but then, what if you decide that you do not really like that default Application anymore? Okay, it is worthy of note that most phones today have an application setting menu and option that is dedicated to it by default right in the application settings. However, you can always try to clear out those defaults by simply finding your very default Applications, which are in the main menu of the app settings. Then, whenever you look at the info page for any Application, there will then be an option toward the bottom for you to view and clear the defaults as you wish. That will then let you select a new default the very next time you want to perform any Application action.

Setting up Developer Options

Google does hide few of the more advanced tools, which are in a special Developer Options menu that you will need to have access to and enable it for you to get at things like animation speed, and even USB debugging, and Application standby too. Actually, to turn on the Google Developer Options, you need to open the "About phone" menu at the very bottom of your device's settings and there, you will have to find the build number. Tap on that seven times, and as you tap on that for seven times, immediately after seven times, you will get a message that you are now an engineer. The dev alternatives will presently be at the very bottom of your main device settings.

These are how these things are done, they are as easy as that, just launch them now and enjoy the smooth sailing of your device.

Chapter 7: Managing your smart watch

Using a smartwatch may become a unique fashion statement in this period of time we live in, although it is also full of fun to use since it does both what a watch does and a fitness band. Several features will allow you to manage calls, or respond to messages, or even get navigation help and even track the state of your health. All of these helpful things can be performed even if your phone is far away from your reach. There are a lot of features that you can try out on your smartwatch, although you need to connect your smart watch to your phone before you can do that. The due process of pairing your phone with an Android Wear watch is actually simple.

One of the things that will be in your mind more will be questions such as; How do I pair my smart such to my Android device, how can I connect it to my iPhone, why is it as though my smart watch is not connecting well with my smart phone and all that. This chapter covers the very initial setup process of smartwatches, including how to customize your watch face and the essential apps you should download. Instructions used here mostly apply to a wide Apple Watches. Android Wear and all other smartwatch platforms. Anyways, for you to pair your smartwatch today, you just need to follow these few steps:

In the Wear Operating System by Google Application on your phone, you will actually see a list of your close by gadgets. You can check the name of your watch on its very own screen. Before you can startup, you must ensure that your watch is charging well. Then you need to Select your language of choice, and as you have, you then need to scroll down to the watch identity. Now, on your phone, you need to touch the name of your watch. If your telephone is now combined with another watch, you can no longer see a pairing code. Rather, you will see a touch Pair With Another New Wearable device and then continue to these steps which are elucidated as seen below:-

- Right down on your watch, you will be opportune to see a pairing code.
- Now, back on your phone, you should see the same very pairing code shown on your watch. Then, you should click on the Pair option. You will be able to see a confirmation message as soon as your watch has been paired to your device. This May take a very few minutes.
- So as you are on your phone, you need to follow the onscreen instructions as fully elucidated to turn on watch notifications, location, and even calendar access.
- If you are pairing your watch after you've done a factory reset of your device, then you will be in dare need to open the Wear Operating System by Google Application on your phone. Then, touch the menu icon, and as you do, select the Pair With New Watch option and then continue with the steps as shown above.

- Downloading the "Wear Operating System by Google - Smartwatch" on your iPhone is a very important step. The application is widely available for free on the App Store.
- After the installation, the next thing for you to do is for you to turn on your Bluetooth on your smartwatch.
- Then you need to go straight on to the Settings on your iPhone and click on the Bluetooth icon. Just wait a little bit till your watch shows up on your iPhone.
- As soon as your smart watch is shown on your device, then you need to click on the watch model you are pairing and then accept the Bluetooth pairing request.
- Once you have paired, you then need to sign in to your Google account.
- Then Enable notifications, location access, and then messages, calendar access, and any other ones available for you to make full proof out of your smart watch.

N/B: You may find out that your watch could automatically install an update and restart after it is paired with your phone. If it starts downloading an update, you will need to keep the phone near as close to your watch as possible and ensure that your watch stays in the charging state until the update is thoroughly finished.

Connecting To An Android Device

In the Wear Operating System by the Google Application on your phone, you will see a whole list of nearby devices. You can then check the name of your watch on its screen. When you've found it, you can click on your watch's name. You will see a pairing code right on your phone and on your watch too. Do try as much as possible to make sure that the codes are of real time match. On the off chance that your telephone is combined with another watch, you will no longer see any pairing code. Rather, you can touch the triangle next to the name of a watch which can be found in the upper left hand corner. Then, you can touch pair with a brand new wearable and then continue to follow the steps shown below:-

- Firstly, you need to click on the Pair option on your phone. Then you will see a whole confirmation message as soon as your watch is paired. This can actually take up to a few minutes, so you need to exercise much patience, please.
- Then, on your phone, you need to Enable Notifications. So click on the checkbox next to Wear Operating System by Google to let your watch show notifications from a whole lot of different applications on your phone.
- You need to Install the "Wear Operating System which is developed by Google Smartwatch" app on your phone, this is actually available on the Google Play Store.
- As you're done with the installation, you need to switch on your watch and turn the Bluetooth on.
- Then you have to open the Wear Operating System Application on your phone and follow the very initial setup. And afterward, click on the "I agree" choice.
- You then should see a pop-up "Turn on Bluetooth and Location." Next, them click on "Turn on."

- Then click on the name of your watch. You will then receive a code on your phone and your watch too. Finally, click the "Pair" button on both gadgets.
- You will presently see a message showing that the connection is successful. You now need to sign in to your Google account.
- When you're done signing into it, you then need to click on "Allow notifications," then "Sync calendar," and "Allow messages," etcetera. For you to be able to proceed to the point of making Adequate use of your smartwatch.

N/B: Your watch may automatically need installations an updates and you really need to restart it after it is paired with your phone.

As soon as the paring and synchronization process is complete, you can then do many tasks such as checking your notifications, getting directions, or even making note entries, with your smart watch, amongst other things. The very best part about Android watches is an in-built Google assistant that is there to simplify your life. You can likewise perform undertakings with simply your voice, contingent upon the gadget you are making use of.

Additionally, you can make use of your smartwatch to track the state of your health and checkup on your fitness goals, listen to your favourite music or even get to find new music from the Google Play Music platform. In addition, you can also make payments with Google Pay when you shop or use it to keep your gift cards, or your loyalty points, or your tickets or even the coupons you get.

Setting Up a Smartwatch

You need to follow these steps in order for you to set up your smartwatch:

- You need first to connect your device to the charger included to it so that you start with a full battery.
- Then you need to download the appropriate app for you to connect your smartwatch with your cell phone. For instance, you need to download the wear app from the Google Play Store on Android watches.
- Then you need to connect the smartwatch to your phone through Bluetooth as explained earlier. Then you need to Enable Bluetooth on your phone, you should then see your smartwatch pop up as an available device. Select it for you to connect.

Customizing a Smartwatch

You can actually download a brand new watch face for you to add some more personality to your device. Several watch faces are available on your watch's mobile app, but you can also get them from third-party applications just like Facer. You can also find a whole part of countenances, from simple plans to faces that show the current climate notwithstanding the time too. Most smartwatch manufacturers also make sales of multiple straps, so if you get bored of the default option, you can buy a steel band, leather, or a totally different color. So you need to enable notifications on your watch for you to get messages and other incoming updates from your phone.

Basic Smartwatch Apps

Aside from text notifications and even Google Now updates (for Wear users), applications really dominate your smartwatch experience. You'll find out that many of your favorite applications are now viable with smartwatches. For example, Instagram chips away at the Apple Watch, while IFTTT and iHeartRadio are completely viable with Wear. Google Play has a devoted Wear area, and the Application Store has an Apple Watch category too. Pebble users can find enormous compatible apps via the Pebble app on their phones.

If you are in dare need of some few ideas to start you off with, then consider downloading a fitness app to track your workouts, or a weather app, even a note-taking app just like Evernote. Once you have some of these good apps, you can then specify which notifications you want to receive on your smartwatch.

How is going? I hope that you are enjoying. It took me a a lot of time to make searches and find something really useful..

Leave a short review on Amazon if you enjoy it.

https://www.amazon.com/review/create-review

Section 2

Chapter 8: Unlocking the full potential of your devices

Of no doubt, your Android phone is way higher and more powerful than you have ever realized. So let us look at some of the things that made the smart phone awesome and how we can unlock them all for our productivity.

Your Android phone has so much more processing power than even a mainframe computer from a few years ago. Access now had access to more than a million Applications, but are you making the most useful application out of it? From a very fast way to delete your messages to even a cooler new functions which you never dreamt of or imagined, so let me briefly take you through on how you can actually unlock your handset's full potential.

Blocking calls from people you don't want

It may be a clingy ex or even a bill collector, it somewhere else that you want to avoid, Android, as well as other smart phone, can help you block any number from getting to you. For example, on a Samsung phone, you can actually put people on your rejection list, which you can do by navigating to the phone's Settings and click on the Call option and then on Call Rejection and finally on Auto Reject List and here, you can keep on adding the numbers of people you don't want calling you, or you can also add them from your contacts. On stock Android devices such as Google Nexus 6, you actually have to edit the contact you don't want calling you by opening the Settings Application and then checking on "All calls to voicemail."

Turning your phone into a hotspot

There is no just need for you to pay extra in order to get your laptop or tablet on 4G when you can turn your phone into a hotspot, true, your can actually use your phone as a hotspot and come out of any monthly fee. Some of the carrier plans do offer this ability for no additional charge, but others may always want you to pay a monthly fee. But install FoxFi on your device, which is a $7.95 app. You then can be able to share that connection with every other devices either wireless or via a direct USB connection, even without incurring extra charges. You can check the latest notes in the Google Play store before you install this particular Application because some carriers have blocked the wireless functionality and work only over USB.

Unlocking your phone with just a Bluetooth device

The lock screen of your phone is duly supposed to protect your data from those prying eyes. However, typing in a password every single time you get out your handset is a time-consuming process. Now new in Android 5.0 and above, Smart Lock lets you designate anything as "trusted devices" — such as headsets or even vehicle frameworks or smartwatches — which keep your telephone opened as long as they are associated with your telephone. In other for you to set this up, you need to get to the Security tab, also referred to as Lock Screen in certain devices such as Samsung, menu in Settings, tap Smart Lock and choose one or more Bluetooth devices for you to trust. If you happen to choose a wearable device and your phone is lost or stolen, it will lock as soon as it is out of range of that device.

Opening the visited Web pages in your web browser when you have no internet connection.

I must have to pause a little bit here to write you once more that you are actually reading a really crucial and timely book, and you may want to finish it first, but you must have to get on the subway too, this is where there is no signal at all or any regular network. But fortunately, there is a way to load a cached version of any of the page you have ever visited recently in Chrome. You can navigate to chrome://flags#show-saved-copy and make changes to the alternative to "Empowered: Primary." You'll then, at that point, see a Saved Copy button when you can visit a Web page you have seen before and you can not load it.

How to decrease or increase the font size of your

It may not matter whether you find the text that is on your screen too small to read or you really need them to shrink, in hopes of fitting in more content on your display screen at once, you can then try to tweak the font size of your texts which show in the display panel of your device to make that to happen. So now, go to the Display menu which you can find under your Settings, and there you will be able to see the Font Size Options or property and, on certain phones — such as the Samsung devices, or Tecno handsets, etcetera — you will be able to make choices to several different font faces.

Listen to any radio network for free.

Everyone knows about certain music streaming services such as the popular Spotify and Rhapsody and even Slacker, but do you actually know that you can hear certain live streams directly from real-time AM and FM stations right on your phone? Yes you truly can. Just download the TuneIn application, and here you can choose from 100,000 different stations that are all around the world, including the wideESPN, BBC Radio, and even NPR.

How to find or wipe the data of a lost phone.

If at all or happens that your phone is lost, missen or stolen by theft, then you can quickly locate it, else, you can lock it, or you can also make it ring at q very full volume by using your Android Device Manager, it is a free Application and an associated Web tool from Google. Ask you need to do is just for you to download the phone app from Google Play, then you would need to enter your Google account information and then you will need to visit this web address; https://www.google.com/android/devicemanager, then when you do so, whenever your device is missen for whatsoever reason, then you can quickly recover it. Most of the third-party Applications offer several similar functionality, but Google keeps it so so simple by making use of your username and your password too.

How to connect your smart device to a mouse, or a keyboard or an SD card reader.

You may actually have a need to type your emails with a cool and real QWERTY keyboard or try to scroll around Web pages with a mouse similar to the mouse of a PC rather than making use of your fingers. The very micro-USB port you use for charging your phone Actually can also connect your device to peripherals. You just can attach a $5 USB OTG cable — or "On the Go" cable, which has a micro-USB male jack that plugs itself directly into your device and a female USB port you can also make use of too for you to connect to other devices like keyboards, or mice or even flash drives. Although it may happen to be that your phone probably may be emitting enough electricity, which will be used to power a wireless mouse or even an SD card reader on its own, technology experts recommend using a powered USB hub for anything else.

Turning your old phone into a real security camera.

As soon as you make the necessary upgrade to a brand new phone or even tablet, your old device can still be serving, it can serve you an important purpose. For you to make use of your old device as a security or surveillance camera, you just need to install AtHome Video Streamer on that your old device which you wish to use as a security camera, then you need to put the AtHome Camera app onto the other phone — the new one — which you want to use for viewing. Then you need to diligently follow all the instructions given for you to follow, which involves taking a picture of a QR code, which will help you pair the two. You can also decide to watch from a PC from anywhere.

Unlock the full potential of your Android device through Rooting

Do you really want to be a super user of a Smart phone like Android? Then if you are an Android user, you probably would have heard about Rooting. It is actually a technical term that sounds so very hard but is just something that a casual smartphone user can get right into and find something beneficial for their device. Although while trying to unlock the full potential of your Android phone, you might also make the warranty of your device to be void or even, it may leave you with a faulty or brick device. Anyways, let us briefly look at the benefits as well as the risks that come with it.

What then is Rooting?

Rooting is just like jail-breaking for Android and it has a way that allows users to dive deeper into a sub system of the Android device. It will fully grant you full access to the entire OS, granting you the opportunity to customise just about everything and anything on your android device. It will also fully walk around any form of restrictions that the device manufacturers had implied, giving you fill and absolute features just like making you able to run much more apps, also allowing you to overclock or under-clock the processor, replace the firmware, and do virtually anything. All you just need to do is back up the current software and install a bend new custom ROM modified for an android version.

Rooting and benefits that come with it

The first thing there is for you as a benefit is that you can get rid of certain bloatware — that unwanted serial software included by the manufacturers, which is impossible for you if you try to uninstall it. You can also install so many special Applications and install several custom ROMs which can help to boost the overall performance of your devices, take for instance, if your phone is struck with an Android device that is of an older version compared to it, and it is not getting any form of update, then with the custom ROM, you could load up that very latest Android version with doing much ease. You can also do a manual procedure of accepting or deny Application permissions. Yet again, you could also set up wireless tethering even if it has been unavoidably disabled by default in your device.

Rooting and risks that comes with it

You might tend to end up making the warranty of your mobile device to be totally void and invalid, some manufacturers or mobile carriers will definitely make use of rooting as an excuse to devoid your warranty. But you also need to keep it in your mind that you can unroot anytime just by simply flashing or installing the backup ROM you already made. Rooting might actually introduce some certain TRI m risks in the security of your device, depending on what services and/or Applications you install and often use on your device.

You run at the very least risk whenever you tamper so so much that it might even lead to bricking your device — making it faulty and even screwing up your device software that it would never run properly and appropriately as it should. Therefore, to avoid any form of bricking, you just need to follow the instructions given and ensure that the instructions you are following work well with your device, and you won't miss any step. So, go ahead and do some research to avoid bricking your device completely.

Every one device has its and their very way and method of rooting them. You just need to search about your device on Google — your Device model and it's name, and this you will do by search the term root on the Google search bar. Let's take for instance, the model of your device is Samsung Galaxy S10, just search about this device and ask Google how you can root it, find it's procedure and follow them meticulously. You will be able to get the steps there. I wish you fun and an enjoyable rooting and unleash the full potential of your device.

Chapter 9: Controlling Your devices remotely

Android as a technological platform is a very diverse platform. It is not limited and restricted to a particular device. It is not only installed on smartphones, but it appears on tablets too, also on set-top-boxes, and also can be installed on smart watches, and can also be installed even in Google Glass. You will also be shocked to set your eyes on it, looking at it running in an emulator on the Operating System developed by Chrome developers, and it is known as Chrome OS. You can also see it as adding Android Applications support to Google's web-centric operating system for laptops and desktops. Android also can be seen being supported by Windows 10, it also allows users to pair their Android phones in other to make calls, to send text messages, or even for them to retrieve their photos, and also be able to see their notifications right on a Windows PC — Operating your Android device from the computer as though you were operating your phone

Anyways, Google—of no doubt—is the very basic foundation. Google stands between the Chrome browser, which is installed on multiple devices and bridges it. Google bridges between Android phones and smart devices like Chrome-cast and Google Home, it can even concert one to another. Google also navigates whenever you connect an Android phone to a car with Android Auto. Android is a major component in the overall services of Google as a company-first initiative that's accessible on all platforms. What Google lacks as a platform is a truly unified messaging experience around devices, as seen on Apple's products. There are so many ways your devices can be controlled remotely, a smart watch can be controlled by a smartphone as we have seen and vice versa, a smartphone can control a PC and vice versa, one Android can control the other and give versa. But here, we'll be seeing how a smartphone can be used to play multimedia remotely and see how a TV can control it and use the resources it provides.

Setting up the Android TV Remote Control app

You can do this by navigating to your Android TV using your phone or tablet with the Android TV Remote Control Application, which is available in the play store. It is worthy of note that you need an Android device that is running Android 4.3 or higher for you to make use of the Android TV Remote Control Application.

Setting up the remote control app

- Now, on your phone, download the Android TV Remote Control app from the Play Store.
- Then connect your phone and Android TV to the very same Wi-Fi network.
- On your phone, you then need to open the Android TV Remote Control app Android TV Remote.
- Then click on the name of your Android TV.

If it doesn't show up at all, then try the troubleshooting steps as shown below:-

- A PIN will have to show on the screen of you Television.
- Now on your phone, you need to enter the PIN. And then, tap Pair.

Adding another User to Your Android Tablet

Computers possess the very capability to allow several users for some time — even though people do not often seem to use this feature. Your Android tablet should be the same, but your tablet can have more than one user account just as your computer is to help for remote actions.

Some tablets permit people to configure multiple users — several people who can have their own unique and customized Home screens or widgets, and even some other options on a single tablet. So, for you to add a new user, just follow these steps as shown below:-

- Firstly, open the Settings app of your tablet and choose Users.
- On a Samsung tablets, you can look on the General tab for the Users item, that's where you will find it.
- If you seem not to find the Users category, your tablet probably may not have this feature, but if it does, then move over to the next step.
- Click on the Add User button.
- Read the information and click on the OK button.
- Go sleep on ahead and configure the new user.
- Then click on the Set Up Now button for you to be able to configure the user, or even better, hand the tablet to the other user and let that person configure it. The whole procedures for the configuration are basically the same setup procedure you passed through when you first turned on the tablet as we used an instance of starting a newly purchased android phone from it's purchase till it is ready to use (See ' overview of my devices').
- All accounts there are on the tablet will have to appear at the very bottom of the lock screen.
- So in order for you or anyone to make use of the tablet as a specific user, then you need to click on the account circle on the lock screen.
- You then can Apply a PIN or any password at all to your account if you have multiple users on a single Android tablet.
- The tablet's first user is actually the main user, the one who has primary administrative control.
- When you're done using the tablet, then you can lock the screen, then the other users can then access their own accounts.
- You can remove an account by visiting the Users screen in the Settings Application. Then you can click on the Trash icon next to an account to remove it. And then click on the Delete button to confirm — permanently deleting it.

Remotely controlling your PC.

If you really want to do something — to get a job done — on your Windows PC but you are far away from your desk, then you can actually control the computer directly through your Android phone — interesting, Right! A number of apps provide remote access, Chrome Remote Desktop is the best and is highly preferable. In order for you to make use of it, then you must install the Chrome Remote Desktop extension on your PC by making use of the Chrome browser, you then need to follow all the setup prompts and then install the companion app on your handset, but make sure as much as possible that your PC is set up so it never goes to sleep.

Chapter 10: Making certain basic installations

Your Smartphone is what you make out of it, and in fact, one of the simplest ways to customize and add new features to your Android phone and other smartphones is by downloading apps. Even if you have the very best Android phone, it won't do you much good without the right applications. There are many applications that are scattered here and there, readily available for your Android device, and by installing new ones, you just have to follow a fairly simple process. In this post of this awesome book, we will briefly look into how a user can walk through the step-by-step means to ensure he know exactly how to find and download the very latest apps to his dear device.

If you do find yourself itching to try a new Application, then you will really want to head over to the Google Play Store. This is the official way to discover and download Android apps, and the dining thing is that the process for installing a new one is about as simple as it could ever be. You can actually download mobile applications for free, although there are also paid apps both from Google Play on your Android phone. It is duly recommended that you get and install your applications directly from Google Play, but you can also get them from specific other sources. Your phone has a security setting known as Google Play Protect, and Google Play Protect help so much and so well to checks for any potentially harmful apps, it warns you any it, and it also does all there is to removes apps if necessary. So, for you to install any application from Google Play Store, just fille these steps as below:-

Downloading Applications from Google Play

The primary way you will install your Applications on Android is by hitting up the Play Store app, which is right on your phone or tablet. You will find the Play Store in your Application drawer and very less likely on the default screen of your home page. You can also open it up by tapping on the shopping bag-like icon at the top-right corner of the app drawer. As soon as you've launched the app and you're in the store, just browse or search for an app and tap the Install button to install it. Let's see how it is done in full details.

- The vert first thing you need to do is go to your application list and select and open Google Play.
- Right on your phone, use the Play Store app Google Play. Or if your on your PC, then go to play.google.com.
- Now seek and find the very application you want — which you either have in mind or saw to be so appealing to your eyes.
- To check that the application is reliable and working well, you have to find out what other people say about it.
- Right under that particular title of that Application, check the star ratings and the number of downloads and the feedback people left there, it will help your choices.
- For you to read individual reviews that people have already made, you need to scroll to the "Reviews" section.
- When you then pick the very Application you need, the next thing to be done is for you to click on Install — is the Application is a free one or if it is a premium plan — if it is a paid application, then you have to put in your credit card details or pay with pay pal.
- You can also Report bad Google Play apps directly to Google. If you find an app that you think is very harmful, then you need to report it to Google.

Downloading Applications from other places

Google provides a primary but essential app store for Android, known as Google Play. Google Play isn't the only game in town, and there are other ways to install apps on Android. Some Android devices — particularly those that are dirt-cheap, coming directly from manufacturers in China — are not really certified by Google and do not include Google Play. This makes the device much less useful, but you can still install apps on it.

It is so worth not that if you download applications from unknown sources, your phone and personal information can be very high. Your phone may be damaged in the process or lose the data you've stored in your device. Your personal information could be harmed or hacked or tempered with.

Downloading From Sideloading Apps

Android OS does support side-loading, this actually allows you to install apps from outside of Google Play. However, this is disabled by default for security reasons. But if you wish to enable it — enable side-loading — all you just need to do is for you to open the Settings app on your Android OS, as soon as you do, click on the Security category, and there enable the Unknown sources check box.

Note here that this can be a real security risk, as it could allow installation of those applications that are not from the Play Store, which could potentially contain malware. So if you enable this setting, it is not less on you to install applications responsibly — try as much as you can to stay away from pirated games and other apps that may contain Android malware.

After enabling this particular setting, then you can download an Android app in an. APK format and install it into your device. Let's take for instance, you could download the. APK file in the default browser of your Android phone and as you do, you open it from the Downloads folder. You could also download the APK file into your computer, then you copy it right over to your Android's file system with a USB cable, then you use a file manager app to browse for it, and tap the APK file to start to initiate the installation process.

Sideloading also allows you to be able to install a variety of apps that are not actually available in the Play Store, some of those Applications are apps such as the XBMC Media Center which is for Android, some various emulators that have been removed from Google Play, and even third-party app store apps just like the Amazon Appstore which is for

Android and Humble Bundle app.

This option may not actually be available in some devices if the manufacturer of the device or the carrier has disabled it. Once certain time AT&T did this, but it has become so much less common. Most devices should have the Unknown sources checkbox so as the user to either tick out leave it.

Third-Party App Stores

Of more importance, Android permits users to go for third-party app stores. The most well-known and popular one amongst others is Amazon's Appstore for Android, which gives away a free paid app every day. The Appstore of Amazon, which is used for Android, is also used natively on Amazon's Kindle Fire devices.

The popular Humble Bundle, which remains popular and sells bundles of indie games for Linux OS, Windows OS, and Mac OS, has also sold Android games. If you purchased any of these games that are gotten in Humble Bundle, containing Android games, you could install the Humble Bundle app and use it to manage the installation and updating of your Humble Bundle games like that. So to either use the Amazon Appstore, or the Humble Bundle, or any other third-party app stores, you will really need to side-load the app store's Application.

Some devices may also come with their own, as it is integrated into third-party app stores. Let's take an instance, Samsung devices usually come with the Samsung Apps Application, which may contain some free versions of some paid apps, but is otherwise fairly uninteresting definitely. And carriers have distributed their own very app stores with their Android devices in the past, but this is becoming very very less common.

Similarly, you should be very careful when side-loading apps, that is how you should be even more careful when using third-party app stores. For instance, you can probably trust Amazon and the Humble Bundle, but you should beware of certain other app stores which are suspicious. Just take this instance, an untrustworthy app store distributing is distributing some pirated applications and may be a source of malware, so it is so recommended that you stay away from those.

Downloading Apps From Your PC

You are also permitted to side-load Applications into your Android device in done other ways, one of which is, if you have an APK file on your computer, you may make use of the excellent AirDroid app to upload it right into your Android device and install it all at once without even connecting your Android device to your computer.

Also, if you're an app developer, you can make use of the adb command — Android debug bridge command — for you to "push" an app to a connected device, you will then make you to install it from your computer. The appropriate command is as follows, where D:\app.apk is the path to the APK file on your computer:

ADB install D:\app.apk

You are also opportune to install Android apps on your Windows PC, which opens up a new world of whole touchscreen games and unique apps on touch-enabled Windows 8 or 10 devices.

Section 3

Chapter 11: Improving your productivity with your devices

You can do many basic skills and tricks with your Mobile and smartphone to boost your productivity. Most of us do spend a whole lot of time on our phones doing nothing that can be productive to our work and to our mind, instead of using them to get things done appropriately. There are many ways you can average l actually use your phone to boost your productivity. Here in this chapter, I will tell you things you can do with your phone and devices that can lead you to get more done with your day.

The very premise of owning a smartphone and the comfort it comes with it is that it makes you a better, drugged and more productive person. Smart phones combine a medley of technologies and features into a single and unique device — phone, messaging, and navigation all included, as well as music player, and alarm clock, and so much more, and all of this awesome feature should actually make you better, it should equip you for almost anything. Of a truth, that is not the reality we see. Most of us spend too much time mindlessly staring through that awesome screen and not getting stuff done.

The good news still remain that your phone can really make you do much more productive than you could ever imagine — you just need to use it more thoughtfully. Let me take you through some ways you can noticeably increase your productivity with your smartphone.

- **You can make use of your phone for better time management and task scheduling lifestyle**. If I may ask, How well me how good are you at making properties of tasks and accomplishing your to-do list? If you have ever been in dare need of some structure as to how you approach your day, you really might want to try your hand at one of the many common time management techniques that rely on scheduling blocks of time to accomplish tasks throughout the day. Let's take for instance, the Pomodoro Technique is a very brilliant and popular strategy that breaks your day and divides it into 25-minute chunks. You then can try to install a Pomodoro Application just like Focus Booster or even PomoDoneApp. You can then make it simple and skip applications wholly and simply use your phone's timer to chunk up your day.
- **Secondly, you can make dare use of the search bar of your phone to get results.** You can search for anything and everything. You probably may have been wasting a whole lot of time as you try to find things on your phone, from your Application list down to your contacts and even down to your calendar entries. But actually, the built-in search tool can serve you a lot, it can discover a wide range of things for you more rapidly than you ever can. There is really no need to find the

calendar app, open it, and start looking for an upcoming appointment. This is also very true about contacts, email messages, and even text messages, your Application list, your file manager, and even the websites. For instance, if you have an iPhone, Spotlight Search is even more powerful than an Android's search bar; it can do simple mathematics without opening the calculator.

- **Also, you can allow your phone to read anything aloud to you.** You should try as much as possible not to be looking at your phone while driving — it is very very dangerous and often illegal. But you can truly reclaim that lost time by having your phone read so loud to you. Talking to and with you. This is almost a feature that is entirely unknown to some settings and some devices. Still, the iPhone and Android can peruse any screen resoundingly — messages, instant messages, website pages, application screens, and even Kindle books. You need to turn the element on in the Settings application; for iPhone as a point of instance, you have to click on the "General" tab of the settings Application and then also click on "Accessibility," then on "Speech," and finally turn on "Speak Screen." Now, for you to get your phone to read anything out loud, you then need to swipe down with two fingers from the highest point of your device on any screen — for iPhones.

- **You can also delete your worst time-sucks.** There are countless advances you need to pass through before you can delete an Instagram account on an iPhone. There is actually no shortage of statistics that tells us that we waste an enormous amount of time on our phones daily. One recent survey expressly found out that the average internet user spent two hours and 22 minutes on social networking and messaging platforms. If that really describes you, then it shows you already know that it can be challenging to moderate your use of social media (don't it?) — the entire experience is truly engineered to be addictive. Now, what is the solution? It's just for you to Delete social media apps from your phone altogether so as to give you a better forced to rely on your computer for that kind of time-waster. Try to imagine what you could accomplish by just getting two hours a day back.

- **Also make use of Pocket to share websites with your computer easily.** There is no doubt that you often run across articles and websites that you need to even spend much more time with and need to save for later. But if you currently email these links to yourself, there's a much better way. Pocket is an application for Android which you can access from the store, and it does allow you to save web pages with just a single tap. At once, they are automatically saved to your Pocket account, which syncs with the Pocket plug-in, which is for Firefox browsers back on your computer.

- **Also get centered by just a very simple meditation.** Your phone usually forms part of the Grand Central Station of distractions and multitasking. But before you think, just for once, let it help you to relax the way you should and center yourself. Using a mindfulness Application just like The Mindfulness App or even Calm, you can set aside anywhere from 3 - 30 minutes a day to conduct guided meditations and reset amid your busy lifestyle.

- **Also make use of Do Not Disturb mode.** Another way for you to find your Zen — and then for you to work more effectively — is for you to shut out the entirety of your telephone's typical interruptions. If you need an hour to work continuously without phone calls, or even text messages, and any other notifications taking your eyes away from your project, then simply turn on Do Not Disturb mode. You can manually enable Do Not Disturb on the iPhone by just pulling down the Control Panel right from the top right of the screen and then tapping on the quarter moon icon. The process is similar on Android too: just pull down from the top and then find the "Do Not Disturb" quick-access button.

- **Also Sync notes with your desktop computer.** Your phone and your desktop computer exist ordinarily in separate universes — it's not easy to share notes and documents between them even without emailing yourself. By moving right down to the cloud, however, you can generally approach similar archives regardless of where you are or what gadget you are making use of. For notes, you may consider Microsoft OneNote or its popular alternative Evernote. Both of this very one keep track of everything you write and bring them in sync between your computer and phone. For everything else — documents, spreadsheets, and even introductions — use Google Docs or simply store your Microsoft Office documents in a cloud administration like Dropbox or OneDrive.
- **Make use of a better keyboard.** If you want to type faster on your phone, if you find default smartphone keyboards too slow and clunky, you need to investigate downloading an alternate one. Android clients have for quite some time had the option to exploit the wonderful Swype console, and it so results accessible for iPhone clients as well. With Swype and TouchPal, you keep your finger on the screen. You swipe your way through the word, moving from one character to another as though it were an Ouija board, truly magnificent If you've never attempted it, Swype sounds peculiar. Yet, it's incredibly simple to learn and can explicitly increase your typing speed.
- **Also allow white noise to soothe you while you work.** Working in a noisy office or just finding it really hard to deal with any form of incidental distractions while you're trying to concentrate well? You are actually a very good candidate to work with soothing white noise in the background. White noise can mask a whole lot of background sounds and improve your core interest. You just need to search for "white noise" in Spotify to get access to all sorts of white noise tracks there are,

including traditional white noise "static," and nature sounds like rain and waterfalls included too.

- **Try to listen to podcasts too.** When you are in the car, your first impulse might be to play music right? But your commute time, on the other hand, is a golden opportunity to learn something new by digging into podcasts. There are a lot of awesome podcasts on business, productivity, and personal growth. Actually, with much in excess of a half million web recordings accessible for testing, you can likewise enjoy a reprieve from all that and pay attention to a digital broadcast that can really gift you the satisfaction you need to quench your curiosity and teach you something.

- **Download the apps your team makes use of instead of logging in via your browser.** It always said, "Unless you're a salmon, don't fight the current." See if your organization uses tools like Trello, or like Slack, or even Google Hangouts, you need to install the appropriate apps on your Smartphone. Just having the app installed means that you don't need to log in via your web browser each time you need to use it on your phone. Most importantly, you'll instantly see notifications when something needs your consideration, and you can convey or oversee projects from anyplace with only a couple of taps.

- **Also make use of your phone to keep tabs on your competition.** In conclusion, if you are in the business world, you can actually put your phone to work keeping tabs on your competition. Likewise, you can utilize web-based media applications like Twitter and Facebook to help watch how contender organizations draw in with clients and utilize online media influencers or even convey their brands. You can likewise attempt however much as could be expected to fabricate a bunch of connections to contender sites or introduce applications that keep you insider savvy on your opposition's news and exercises. Fondly, you need to stay on the very top of them when you are on the go to help inform your strategy whenever you are back at your desk.

Chapter 12: Being safe with your devices

Smartphones, as well as mobile devices, are inevitably part of our day to day life. And recently, according to statistics, there are about 5 billion mobile subscribers in the whole world. This shows that most of the world's population owns a smartphone or at least any mobile device. Not withstand the fact that smartphones provide greater and better convenience in our daily lives. However, it could also cause serious health issues due to long-term exposure of electromagnetic radiation, which forms the basic means of communication between these devices. How about we perceive how to utilize cell phones and cell phones securely.

Do Avoid long conversation

Long conversation (long-calls) that is done without applying property health measures — using appropriate headphones — causes a heating and damaging effect on brain cells due to the impact of electromagnetic radiation. Radio Frequency radiation could actually permeate human cells and damage tissues in our body over time. In fact, long-term exposure to high power Radio Frequency signals could harm our brain cells, skin, ear, and others.

The short-term effect of Electromagnetic radiation in individuals differs tremendously; some feel a warm headache, others are tired and yet a few others feel dizziness, etcetera. So during cell phone conversation, it is crucial to reduce movement and make it as little as possible.

Make use of headset options

A good and nicely wired or wireless headsets reduces the risk of electromagnetic radiation to the brain cells. So try as much as possible to make use of speakerphone options whenever possible. On the other hand, Bluetooth technology makes use of very low power for transmission and is considered a safe way to use mobile devices.

Keep mobile devices away from the body

All devices that are transmitting a wave should be keep far away from your body. Avoid any direct contact with your body and keep it inside a bag or a pouch if possible. While sleeping, make sure to keep your mobile devices away from your bed and switch off your mobile data as well as your Wi-Fi options. Cell towers always and consistently send ping signals to mobile devices to keep track of them so far as the UE is still under cell circle. So as much as it lies on you, make sure your cell phone has a safe SAR rating by its manufacturers.

Turn off Your WiFi and Cellular data

You need always to turn off the cellular data and the WiFi option of your phone and even the bluetooth connection whenever it is not in use. Before you go to bed to sleep, make sure to turn off all wireless transmitting devices like wireless routers, you'd you can do this by using a timer or just by manually offing it.

Most of the time, mobile devices are connected to wireless data at home and even in our place of work — in our offices. Those applications used on mobile devices are continuously running in the background; so turn off the data and Wi-Fi option to stop them from communicating.

Avoid Making calls at low signals

In order for mobile devices to keep connected with mobile tower, they increase their transmission power if the signal reception is poor. So however much as could be expected, attempt to stay away from places where signal reception from mobile tower is very poor. For example, try to avoid basements and underground parking stations and also in elevators due to poor signal reception. You need to avoid phone calls while traveling on a vehicle too. This is because cell phones continuously send signals to keep in touch with cell pinnacles and make the cell phone send high force radiation than normal or idle conditions.

Make fewer calls, send More Texts

Sending text messages takes a shorter transmission time and is even safer than long conversations. So it better to use text messages or email messages whenever possible so as to avoid mobile phone calls as much as possible. This is because text messaging allows us to keep the cell phone far away from our body the very easy it is needed and a shorter duration of the transmission is always much safer than longer calls.

Use landline telephones rather

Calls made using landline telephones are in short, the safest way to communicate, it reduces the use of mobile phones and cordless phones. Make use of landline phones if you're in your office and at home for very long conversations. Most professionals make a choice of a landline number as a preferred medium for business calls instead of mobile numbers.

Keep phone away from children's reach

Children are so sensitive to Radio Frequency radiation than sent adults due to their head's smaller circumference and brain size. Previous studies show that cell phone radiation affects bone density and is felt more, especially in kids beneath the age of 10 years of age. So in this way, don't permit your youngsters and some other kid to utilize cell phones except if truly important and settle on sure the decision length is pretty much as short as could really be expected.

Radiation protection accessories

Today, several products in the market with claims of electromagnetic radiation protection up to 75% and 90%, etcetera. In reality, these are not as effective as advertised since transmission of electromagnetic waves is inevitable for devices to maintain communication to their cell base stations. The best solution is to avoid health risks by practising a very mild smartphone and other mobile devices.

The place of Safe Charging

Always try to use original chargers provided by phone manufacturers to avoid hazard of electric shock. Also, try to avoid the use of a phone and wired headset while charging. There have been some accidents Report earlier, which happening during charging of devices. Therefore, quick charging arrangements in the market may not be a very good idea unless recommended by the device manufacturers.

Measures to avoid Device Fraud

With the invention of cellular telephones and it's integration into other functions, what has become a multifunctional device, this device does offer so many opportunities to support the commission of a high-technology crime as the target or the "victim," and this is really a tool to be used by certain rascals to commit high-technology crimes. Those drones which are so related to cellular phones cannot be so eliminated, but they can actually be reduced if some simple steps are taken. Some of these steps include the following:-

- Do ensure that cellular phones are fully and adequately justified.
- Also, establish and also enforce every good security policies and procedure that are needed.
- Briefly educate phone users on security requirements.
- Always approve phone numbers to be called, and this should be done in advance.
- Try to limit call areas to those which are only required for business.
- Do coordinate with those cellular phone providers so as to establish billing thresholds for you.
- Also, secure the phone out of sight whenever it is not in use.
- Do not make a call if you suspect anyone or sense suspicious people and activities near you.
- Also, always make use of encryption when possible so as to protect your sensitive information.
- And Actively monitor all the billings and verify the legitimacy of the calls.

Conclusion

Progression in any advances is intended to make for our benefit and wellbeing. It is our duty to ensure that the utilization of innovation won't hurt people and nature. Rehearsing of security strategies is huge for a sound way of life and ensure our other living creatures.

Android is so customizable and versatile. Devices have made our world better, our work easier and our relationships closer. In this book, we saw the comparison of the Operating Systems and devices which we make use of, and we also saw how we could switch from iPhone to Android and between other devices — with complete instructions for moving your music, photos, and contacts — as well as how to back them up. A guide was also given on how to stay healthy with your device, be productive with it, and maximize all the good potentials that come with all the devices we have.

In case you're holding your gleaming new Android cell phone and considering how to take full advantage of it, then, at that point, you've gone to the opportune spot. The advantages of utilizing an Android cell phone are, for the most part emotional to a person's requirements, yet the overall ones are as per the following.

Android is an incredible working framework that can be utilized for significantly more than simply your ordinary web-based media use, WhatsApp and calling.

Not at all like iOS, Android is endlessly adjustable and is an entirely skilled and amazing OS that can be utilized for a lot more.

Here are lots of things you can do with your Android Phone that you might know about:

1. You Can Sideload Apps From Outside the Play Store

In the event that you can't discover the application that you're searching for in the Google Play Store, you can sidestep it with only a couple of taps on your telephone settings, contingent upon your gadget.

Having an Android cell phone gives you the freedom to introduce non-Play Store applications. Moreover, you are not restricted to introducing simply the best Android applications on Play Store but instead from outsiders too.

Stores like APKPure.com and APKMirror.com are acceptable, and for the most part safe option application stores that you can use on basically any Android gadget.

The iOS framework restrains you from introducing obscure sources, so you're constantly restricted to what Apple does and doesn't need you to utilize.

2. Bunches of Hardware Innovations

Gadgets with Android frameworks have various equipment arrangements to bring to the table to purchasers. You get your selection of processors, battery sizes, measures of RAM or capacity, and backing for removable capacity like the utilization of memory cards.

Some choices cover a wide scope of sizes, shapes, and capabilities. However, most equipment developments come from Android and include bendy telephones, in-screen unique mark scanners, and spring up selfie cameras.

3. Expandable Memory

Topping off your capacity isn't an issue for some Android telephones with its help for expandable memory. Through removable capacity, for example, memory cards, Android clients can advantageously put extra memory stockpiling to help their requirements. You can save your most loved applications to a memory card, just like photographs and recordings.

Not all telephones support additional memory, however, similar to the Samsung Galaxy S21. On the off chance that your picked model doesn't, ensure it has sufficient capacity for your necessities when you get it.

4. Gadgets

Gadgets are for those applications or data you need to know immediately, like a schedule and its updates, climate gauges, pertinent news features, and significantly more. Some are for getting data rapidly; others offer advantageous controls, for example, for your media applications.

In spite of the fact that iOS cell phones have gadgets, Android's are much more perplexing and skilled. They permit you to get to significant data with minimal measure of looking over and tapping.

5. Various Phone Options

As you probably are aware, Android is a working framework that takes into account a wide scope of cell phone brands across the globe. So naturally, this implies that there is a wide assortment of gadgets to look over.

Each brand offers unmistakable equipment and highlights to mirror its image and target markets. Android cell phones change in size, telephone stockpiling, camera pixels, battery life, style, and that's only the tip of the iceberg. Regardless of what your financial plan or how large a screen you need, you'll discover an Android gadget that suits you.

Android tips are somewhat trickier to offer than iPhone tips, two or three reasons. For one, it's regularly up to transporters or makers - as opposed to shoppers - who have power over which variant of Android your telephone is running. Moreover, there are such countless more sorts of Android telephones, which have their perfect little highlights. For example, my telephone is a Samsung Galaxy S6 (Review | Pictures), yet menu alternatives might be distinctive relying upon what sort of telephone you use.

I've attempted to keep these tips as all inclusive as could be expected.

1) Customize, redo, alter

As I would like to think, the absolute best part about being an Android client is the way that you can play a ton with your telephone to make it your own. Numerous perusers were sent in to say that they like utilizing custom console applications on their Android telephones.

In any case, there's an entire universe of redoing applications out there accessible only to Android telephones. For instance, you can decide to change the manner in which your home screen looks or how your applications are coordinated by utilizing something many refer to as an application launcher. I for one utilize Yahoo's Aviate, which naturally arranges applications by type, season of day and area. So in case, I'm busy working, for instance, it will not put Netflix on my short rundown of applications. On the off chance that it's an ideal opportunity to drive, travel applications may get a more conspicuous charging.

You can likewise download an assortment of diallers and guest ID applications, for instance, to additionally tweak your telephone. Truly, anything is possible for you.

2) Embrace the entirety of Google

Another vital benefit of the Android life is that there's a ton of combinations in case you're a Google client. For example, the center applications, Gmail, Calendar, Photos, and others should work consistently with your telephone. Google's voice collaborator is only an "Alright Google" away.

An especially decent element in the most recent Android form (Marshmallow) is Google Now on Tap, which kind of goes about as a Google-controlled commentary to whatever you're perusing tap a word and you'll get a Google search about it.

In any case, regardless of whether you don't have Marshmallow, you can run a Google search on any expression on any site in Chrome by featuring text. A little window should slide up from the lower part of the screen, and tapping it will start a pursuit. You don't need to leave the page you're on. You can likewise kill this in Chrome's settings. Simply head to Setting> Privacy > Touch to Search.

3) Know what you're sharing

One inquiry I regularly get about applications is the means by which you can perceive what you're offering to them. You can do this by going to your Settings menu and discovering your Applications Manager. Choosing a specific application should give you a rundown of authorizations, alongside a clarification of what they mean.

If you end up having the most recent Android adaptation, you should likewise have the option to get somewhat more authority over the application authorizations. So on the off chance that you need to, for instance, share your area with an application, however, aren't that cheerful about sharing your contact show, you might have the option to turn that off. But, of course, it relies upon the application, too, so this may not work for each program.

4) Mess around with your defaults

Another significant advantage of being an Android client is that you can consequently change applications that handle specific capacities. So on the off chance that you have a program you like or a PDF peruser you truly like, you can utilize it consequently. Likewise, if you'd prefer to consistently see YouTube recordings in the YouTube application rather than on the versatile web, you can do that as well.

It's quite simple to do this; frequently, your telephone itself will inquire as to whether you need to set a default application when you perform different capacities. On the off chance that you adjust your perspective, you can go into the settings for whatever default application you've picked through the Settings menu and pick Clear Defaults.

A few telephones, like the Samsung Galaxy S6, likewise have a menu called Default applications, which will list every one of the defaults you've chosen on your telephone.

5) Track your information use

Stressed over surpassing your information plan? Android telephones ought to have an underlying information tracker that allows you to monitor what you're utilizing. This ought to be in your Settings menu, under the heading like Data utilization.

You can likewise modify this element so it fits with your charging cycle.

6) Disable pointless applications

You may not be wild about each application that accompanies your telephone; frequently, transporters and producers add applications that you essentially will not utilize. Be that as it may, while you can't generally uninstall these applications, you can frequently hold them back from running on your telephone. On Android, you can cripple these applications to hold them back from running behind the scenes. Simply head to your telephone's form of the application supervisor, tap on the application you need to steady, and hit Disable.

On the off chance that you at any point need to re-empower the application, you can do that by following similar advances.

(Likewise see: Five Simple Tips to Increase the Life of Your Phone's Battery)

7) Conserve your battery life

If your telephone has a force saving method or some likeness thereof, you can decide to have it naturally kick in when your telephone's battery hits a specific charge rate. First, head to the Battery part of your Settings menu. Then, if your telephone has a force saving mode choice, go into that element's settings and set it to kick in consequently when your battery's at different force levels. (On my Samsung Galaxy S6, the alternatives are 50, 20, 15 and 5 percent.) That could get you an additional hour or so of battery life when you're coming up short.

(Likewise see: Eight Simple Tips to Increase the Battery Life of Your Mobile Device)

8) Become an engineer to make things run all the more rapidly

In the event that you need to make your telephone move somewhat more rapidly, you can empower its designer choices to speed it up. The cycle to turn on this alternative is somewhat clever; you need to head into the About this telephone menu in your settings, then, at that point, discover the segment that says Build number. Then, at that point - and I'm genuine about this - you tap that thing multiple times.

Congrats, you're currently an engineer! In any event, as indicated by your telephone. You should see another thing spring up in the About menu, called Developer choices. You can change a couple of alternatives inside that menu - specifically Window activity scale, Transition movement scale and Animator term scale - to .5x or lower. This should accelerate your telephone by decreasing the time it spends enlivening advances among windows and applications. On the other hand, this causes things to feel somewhat more sudden when you're exchanging between windows. In any case, recollect: you can generally return it in the event that you have issues.

9) Swipe down for speedy admittance to settings

Need to get speedy admittance to your spotlight? A one-contact alternative for Airplane Mode? Locking the screen pivot? Swipe down from the highest point of your telephone and you should track down the Quick Settings menu. This is a beautiful fundamental apparatus for exploring your telephone, however you'd be astonished by the number of individuals who either don't think about it or fail to remember it.

Numerous perusers likewise sent in to take note of that you can rework which notices show up in this drop-down menu on different telephones - I heard from Samsung, HTC, LG and Nexus clients on this one.

Peruser tips

10) Try outperforming various tasks

A few Samsung proprietors sent in to say that you can run two applications simultaneously on a considerable lot of their more up to date gadgets. To trigger that, you can tap and hold the Recent Apps button on your telephone, which will generally be to one side of the actual home catch. That will incite it to go into split-screen see.

11) Use the Gesture search application

One peruser sent in to rave about Google Gesture Search, an Android-just application that allows you to explore through your telephone with various motions.

"In the event that you need to discover nearly anything on your telephone, you can normally discover it with only a few swipes of your finger," the peruser composed. The application works with a wide assortment of Android gadgets and variants of the working framework.

12) Get fast admittance to the camera

Another Samsung client sent in to share a tip about getting to the camera application quicker. "The Samsung Galaxy 5's fantastic camera is only a swipe away on account of an alternate route that saves a couple of moments typically spent on opening the gadget," she composed. You can empower the alternate route on that gadget by making a beeline for the Lock screen menu in your settings and choosing Camera Shortcut.

Different telephones may have a camera alternate route on the lock screen naturally - investigate! A few telephones may have their particular manners of getting to the camera quickly. Some HTC telephones, for instance, will dispatch the camera on the off chance that you hit the volume up button. Different telephones, for example, the Nexus 6P (Review | Pictures) and Nexus 5x (Review | Pictures), have choices to dispatch the camera with motions.

Android is the most well known versatile working framework for a valid justification. It's not difficult to utilize, has many applications, and is loaded with development. What's more, with costs going from $100 to $1000 or more, it's available to anybody on any financial plan.

Obviously, it isn't great and has imperfections that we'd love to see fixed in the future. Yet, the stage's adaptability implies that regardless of whether you do have issues meanwhile, they're not difficult to fix.

Android is an assorted stage. It's introduced on cell phones as well as shows up on tablets, set-top-boxes, smartwatches — even in Google Glass. You'll likewise see it running in an emulator on Chrome OS, adding Android application backing to Google's web-driven working framework for workstations and work areas. Android is likewise upheld by Windows 10, permitting clients to combine their Android telephones to settle on decisions, send instant messages, recover their photographs, and see their warnings directly on a Windows PC.

Nonetheless, Google is the establishment. Google connects the Chrome program introduced on various gadgets. Google spans Android telephones to keen gadgets like Chromecast and Google Home. Google explores when you associate an Android telephone to a vehicle with Android Auto. Android is a significant part in Google's general administration's first drive that is open on all stages.

We are at the end, if you enjoyed this book like I had the pleasure to write it, please let me know your thoughts with a review on amazon.

Thank you! It will be a pleasure to have you also for my next books.

https://www.amazon.com/review/create-review

Lightning Source UK Ltd.
Milton Keynes UK
UKHW020439031121
393296UK00011B/672